Sacred Journey Africa

Sacred Journey Africa

Reclaiming Your Ancestral Heritage

Tawan Chester PhD

Dumouriez Publishing
Jacksonville, Florida

Sacred Journey Africa –Reclaiming Your Ancestral Heritage

Published by:
Dumouriez Publishing
P.O.Box 12849
Jacksonville, Florida 32209
http//www.dpublishing1.com

Disclaimer & Safety Note:
Take extra precautions when using candles and fire as serious damage can occur. Never leave burning candles unattended. Always use fireproof containers for burning candles because other types of containers can melt or break. Keep burning candles and open flames clear of flammable materials.

ISBN: 0-9764387-63
ISBN13: 978-9764387-62

Dedication

This book marks a change, an awareness, and a turning point in my life's path. I therefore dedicate the essence of it to all that dare to know and live in their true heritage.

Contents

PREFACE

I do not like it when authors emendate you with an enormous amount of filler information. It really is not information it is just a lot of useless ramblings that takes up time. With that in mind I will be as brief as possible. The Editor felt it would be helpful for you to what led me of embark upon my Sacred Journey.

I have not pinpointed the exact time but the root of my motivation has to be part of the healing process or the filling of the void that was left after the passing of my mother. It is approaching the 20th year and it is still very difficult for me to discuss any part of it. Needless to say this has been the hold up with completing this manual.

My mother's actual transition happened quite quickly, too quickly for words. I cannot go into details but her transition not only left a disconnect in my life but a void as well. Only recently was I able to fathom how vast the void was. With sketchy details that I do have, I will say, my father did not follow her but he transitioned from this plane almost six months after my mom had left.

I started reconnecting with my siblings some 18 years later. Me being the only girl of six children, I could not be the glue that my mother was. There was nothing that we could talk about that did not include my mom. I know my siblings all feel that way because we seem to move quickly from one topic to another with awkward amounts of silence in between

In all of those years my mom has come to me occasionally making sure to stay in the outer perimeter of my dreams. She makes her presence known but it was only recently, say in the last three years, that she spoke to me. She reconnected me with a Great-Great Grandmother. With their help and guidance I was able to reconnect with other ancestors and Sacred Journey Africa was born

It is amazing to be able to meet my ancestors and see who I really am. I have learned how to connect with my ancestors and have seen some strange and wonderful things. The information comes through as vividly as if I had been a participant. Some things are understood quite quickly and others take a little longer so that I am able to get the full workings and understanding. This is due to the differences in generations and the way things were done. I do not feel or sense the void anymore.

Since embarking on my Sacred Journey, I seem to have gained a greater awareness of just who I really am and what I am really made of. I'm now in the process of rethinking my life's path. My mom showed me how to think and expand my mental faculties. She also instilled in me the ability to be self-sufficient. She gave me room to grow and show me how to explore the world around me. These maybe the reasons I tell everyone that I can how important it is to read, search out information, and educate yourself as much as possible. Reading really is a fundamental skill and knowledge really is power.

In this country my family possessed invisible ties of love that seemed to have died as each generation transitioned away from this plane. Now it feels as if my family is scattered like dust in the winds. We are a family that takes pride in each other but we have very strong wills. I look forward to the day that this information will help bring restoration to my family but each individual must take to himself or herself knowledge and use it at his or her own pace.

I believe that the time is coming that the affects that the Great Riff has had upon my family will be no more. We will stand and move as a unit and as a people free of the stench and affects of the Great Riff not only in the country but also around the globe. You have been totally cut off from your ancestors. Though a number of people have successfully traced their ancestry back to an African region or tribe, the majority have not.

There exists a lineage that stretches beyond anything that you can imagine. Your true lineage stretches through time, space, and dimensions, but many never make the connection with it because they are unaware of it. Using the various techniques contained within

Sacred Journey Africa you will reconnect with your ancestors. Re-establishing that precious connection will bring strength to you and allow you to move forward in a new way.

PART I

PRELIMINARIES

Chapter 1

Overview

This is a Sacred Journey. It is an investment in yourself, in your future and generations that follow after you. Sacred, because the information is valuable and has meaning for your life. It should be guarded as such and passed on to future generations. There are several statements floating about that hold elements of truth, but are often ignored.

One is, "you don't know where you're going if you don't know where you've been." Many go in circles, repeating mistakes of past relatives when they do not know it has been tried before. Another one states, "A tree cannot truly exist or flourish without the roots." The fact is that a tree would die without its roots; and so it is with African Americans. It appears that they are the only race in the United States of America that have no connection to their heritage.

When other races migrated, they were called immigrants. They brought something from their past, even if it was just a trinket, a photo, traditional behavior, their language or even a name. These were treated as sacred items; they were deemed so special in that they were thought to be essential to the very make up and continued existence of the race. They helped to maintain a connection to that of homeland and past generations while in a new and foreign land.

Those things are the foundations of the families and the race; the things that are passed on through history and time, to build up the future of a race and to help strengthen future generations. Those are the things that were stripped from the African people especially those that were taken to America and the generations of those that were born there afterwards.

They continued to be stripped through generations until who they really were became a faint shadow in the form and sounds of past ages. Their eyes beheld in the mirror the perfect chameleon... the reflection of those around them. So perfect in their disguises, that the sounds that are spoken are also a reflection of those around them. This in itself is a tragedy, but these actions led to a race of people rejecting the very sight and mannerisms of who they truly are.

The society, in which they are members of, rejected every part of them and so to fit and succeed in their society, they followed suit-- rejecting each other as society does, based on appearances of hair texture, skin color, language, speech, dialect, and mannerisms connected to their heritage. This can be seen in almost every place that you look especially in the celebrity arenas.

The irony in all of this is that the same features that are rejected when they appear naturally in African Americans are seen as highly desirable in other races (Caucasian, Hispanic, Asian, etc.). Some even surgically alter their features to mimic those African traits. The medical and tanning industries pull in millions of dollars each year, altering the face and bodies of people that do not need surgery, but have procedures done to look more appealing.

The cosmetic industry does the same thing, but is inferior when it comes to lasting results. What kind of backwards thinking society rejects skin color, facial and body features, hairstyles, language, music, etc. of one race when it is part of their DNA, but accepts it when another race displays it? I will tell you what it is. It is twisted and backwards to put others down, to oppress them for who they are, and then exploit everything about them for power and financial gain.

When you are taught from a child to reject everything about your biological makeup, you cannot accept or love yourself and others like you. If you are not connected to the essence of who you really are, then you lack the driving force that can push you into success.

The people that comprise the African race are elite and of an exceptional quality but it could also be said that they are some of the most gullible. Those of direct African descent maybe the most hated and feared race because of what is locked inside of them. It is their very essence that invokes fear in others. They possess the ability to adapt, overcome, and master any situation posed to them. That maybe the reason there are constant attempts at oppressing, raping, enslaving, stripping, brainwashing, and genocidal interactions with them.

I am making these statements to provoke and sound a call to action as well as thought. My statements are not meant to incite violence through speech or actions upon another person or race, but upon that which you have taken as being part of your being and truth concerning your own race. This is a clarion call for you to take thought and action. Those actions should bring about a restoration of a race and they must start with you. Most of what you know about your own race comes from what your oppressors or those from another race have told you. You have very little knowledge that came from within your race and none from before the Great Rift.

In every generation there are those that echo these same sentiments and some people are moved to take action. We must, however, find a way to not just spark a movement, but also restore and reconnect an entire race of people. A paradigm shift was started some decades ago and it shifted into overdrive within the last decade. Its affects are far reaching and its clarion calls will not go unanswered. If we are able to connect with our ancestors and be restored, we can then connect with others and help them reach a point of restoration.

Eventually, we are able to be restored as a race if we do as our communal ancestors did; moving in a spiritual oneness with the Divine Source of all Creation. Only then can we agree to disagree and accept others as a manifested aspect of our Infinite Being. We would see that we evoke change and action in others. We would not be jealous or envious of another, because of our connections as human beings. We would not reach Utopia, but we would not be living in Hell.

Much of this may seem quite strange to you, but I am sure you have heard about the connections between twins, triplets, quadruplets, etc. There have also been similar reports between mother and children as well as other relatives, lovers and spouses and friends that had close emotional ties. These connections between them were so strong that they could sense when the other person was hurt, in danger, or experiencing other heightened emotions. Some could even sense the loss when another transitioned from this realm.

Those ancestors that came before you have experienced similar emotions in the past when their loved ones suffered tragedies. Husband, wife, mother, father, sister, brother, etc. were captured like animals and led away…never to be seen again and never to return. They searched; they longed, cried, and wrestled with despair only to be swallowed up in a sea of hopelessness. They could not forget…but they remembered and sent prayers, cries, and well wishes into the Universe hoping that they would reach their loved ones wherever they may be. You are one of their descendants.

By embarking on your Sacred Journey you are choosing to reconnect with them and to grant them rest.

Chapter 2

Purpose for the Journey

I hope to help many find a place of center and regain the important things that were stripped away. It is my hope that this information will help many people find a true place of being. This is the place from which you must progress. You will not be presented with direct family information but you can through the use of the techniques presented here gain knowledge concerning your family including their place of origin. You will have a new beginning when you are able to reconnect with that part of you that was lost. This is your heritage that was lost in the shuffle of integrating into a society that was never yours.

Over the centuries, many cultures and societies change by absorbing the people, traditions, and workings that others bring to it. This could be in the form of technology, machinery, entertainment, art, religion, etc. Many African tribes and countries display this today. The problem is that you, as a people, were suddenly and brutally torn from home, people, country, and tradition. You were totally submerged into another society and forced to give up all that made you who you are.

As a people, your survival in the new country depended on you letting go of all that made you a people. You were forced to become a puppet by taking on the mannerisms, behavior, and demeanor of others. A puppet is a lifeless item; moving as the string-master commands. It makes no sound, but, that which the puppet master utters.

After many generations in the new society, the people are still busy trying to adapt to an ever-changing landscape within the society. This means imitating those in power or that hold positions of higher status. Some go so far as to mutilate themselves through surgery by changing their outward appearance to be accepted, or be destructive in their actions and behavior.

Our society is full of people that have lost themselves. They have taken on the mindset and behavioral patterns of chameleons, peacocks, hippos, and hyenas. Many went the way of the chameleon and were ridiculed and labeled "Uncle Tom." Those that took on the peacock's behavior appear as flamboyant billboards that must be seen. The people with hyena type behavior tend to be loudly obnoxious all of the time. Those that are part of the backbone or foundation of the race are seemingly filling the jails because of their hotheaded antics. They are the ones with the hippo behavior and they find themselves in situations they should not be in.

The true you is always trying to express itself. After being suppressed for too long, it will find a way to push back. It will instinctively adapt, scratch, and fight to survive. As an instinctive survival reaction, the true nature of a person may appear as a form of rebellion. In the past these behavior patterns were needed for survival purposes but now the Universe is calling for a change. You must first realize that while you are trying to be like someone else that same someone is trying to be like you.

Instead of making others rich or richer by buying expensive brand name products you can make your own brand and get rich. Look and observe: where the African American dollar flows, riches follow! There are examples that are showing that if you as a people would equip yourself with knowledge you can not only overcome but also excel. You will need to set a goal and map out a logical workable plan with deadlines that will help you stay on track and reach your goal in record time. If you keep your head (thinking) straight and not let emotions lead you then you cannot be denied and great success will be yours.

The Sacred Journey will not solve all of your problems, but it will give you a point from which to work. It can help spark and ignite the much-needed unity in a people. It can help join them together so that they are able to push and encourage one another. They will help to unlock the greatness and the potential in each other so that they are able to leave a legacy for future generations.

Chapter 3

Phases of a Sacred Journey

There are five areas within The Sacred Journey. The phase is the initial act of connecting you with an area. Once the connection in made you can then explore the area. You will connect with the Earth, the African continent, your ancestral tribe, your ancestral family, and Divine Source. You will then travel through the area and explore them so that you can be reacquainted with the land, the customs, and the people.

Phase 1: Connect with Earth
This phase connects you with the area of the Earth to bring knowledge of the atmosphere, environment, and global information.

Phase 2: Connect with the African continent
This phase connects you with the African continent to bring information concerning the African environment, animals and inhabitants

Phase 3: Connect with Tribe
This phase connects you with your ancestral tribe to give you access to communal information and information involving ceremonies, events, initiations, habits, behavior, etc.

Phase 4: Connect with Family
This phase connects you with the many ancestral families that came before you and gives you access to information concerning events, births, deaths, initiations, behavior, training, etc.

Phase 5: Connect with Divine Source
This phase connects you with Divine Source to provide you with information of the purest kind. Whether the information is known, lost, or hidden it is free of unnecessary attachments. This is really just to reopen and reawaken a part of you that is dormant.

Each Connection Phase is essential to your journey and will help restore the bond between you and a part of your past. It will provide you with a completely new perspective of your ancestral past. The connections are conducted in a specific order because each leg of the journey builds upon the previous one.

The information you gain at each area of the journey is used to strengthen your connection at that leg and to move you further along your journey. For instance, the first connection you make is with the Earth. You are a spiritual Being in a physical form. You will use both of those aspects when moving along your Sacred Journey.

When you make the physical connection with the Earth, a vibrational chord is sounded. You cannot hear it unless you are hypersensitive in that area, but you can feel it and sense it. If you do not feel or sense it at first do not worry because you will become more sensitive to the vibrations the more you interact with them. You will then utilize that sensing and feeling to help along the next leg and connect to the African continent.

The awakenings and information that come forth through your connection to the continent can then assist you in making the connection to your ancestral tribe. The tribal information and awakenings then help you connect to your ancestral family. You are able to connect to many generations prior to the "Great Rift." Your Sacred Journey can take you all the way back to Divine Source because it is there that your true heritage lies.

Once you decide these things are doable and you decide to take the Sacred Journey things will start unfolding before you. You may want to make a note of any information that comes to you that has hints of being related to Africa. The techniques or exercises that you use during the Sacred Journey will help you forge a connection and awaken your true spiritual nature.

When you master these you may not have a desire to use the tools presented in this text. If you do not need to use them, by all means, do not. You should, however, try them in the beginning, so that you can see how they are able to assist you. Who knows, you just may find yourself instructing others on how to use them.

Chapter 4

Africa

Our focus starts with Africa for several reasons, but primarily because scientific research has uncovered information that shows Africa is where mankind began and is the "cradle of civilization." Africa is the second largest continent in the world. It is the second most populated continent as of this writing.

The oldest skeletal remains were found in Africa. The adult female fossilized skeletal remains called Lucy, was found in the Awash Valley in Hadar, Ethiopia's Afar Depression, placing it some 3.2 million years ago. The fossilized remains of a three-year-old female called Selam was found in Dikika, Ethiopia (Afar Depression) and was dated about 3.3 million years ago. Ardi is a 4.4 million year old fossilized hominid-like skeleton that was found near the Awash River.

The African continent is also considered to be the oldest inhabited area on Earth. Central East Africa is considered to be the actual birthplace of the human race, according to the carbon dating of archeological artifacts of human remains. The equator runs across it so that it is situated in a manner that causes it to encompass both northern & southern temperatures. It is situated in such a way that the Tropic of Cancer runs across the top portion of the continent with the Tropic of Capricorn running along the bottom portion of it; the equator in the middle. This is a land of extremes in every sense of the word. Unfortunately the extremes have not only occurred in the land but in the people that have trekked the continent as well.

The continent's landscape was quite different long ago. It is hard to imagine this was a lush, green land, flowing with various bodies of water. Africa is a continent that has endured the test of time. Many parts are barren and uninhabitable for humans. It holds one of the largest and harshest deserts in the world. So many areas have been stripped above and below ground of its natural resources.

Living conditions for plants, animals, and humans depend so heavily on the constantly changing seasonal environment. The existence of every species is interconnected and they depend on each other. The smallest change can have an enormous effect on the land and its inhabitants.

Africa is often referred to as the Dark Continent by many. Is it because of the people native to that continent? That could be true, but there is another reason. The continent holds many mysteries. Mysteries are thought of as being dark. Many of the mysteries held by the continent are still hidden and may never be revealed to man. The more the continent reveals of itself, the more we realize there are many mysteries yet hidden.

The answers to most of the continent's mysteries appear to be within our grasp, but the closer we get to obtaining them, the more we notice layer upon mystery-filled layer remains. Lost civilizations, the origins of mankind and other species, land formations, animal migrations, weather patterns, are among the many mysteries of the continent.

Chapter 5

Your Heritage

You came from a people that, not only respected their connection to the Earth and things in the universe, but they embraced them as well. Many ancestors were remembered through ceremony, prayers, folklore, and everyday life. Skills of a craft were handed down from generation to generation.

The entire community depended on the skills and knowledge of its craftsmen. Almost every occasion provided an opportunity to interact with the universe and to provide the intricate inner workings that keep a community thriving. Myths and legends hid truths but often the occasion or celebration signaled the changing seasons or times of migration which were vital to the very survival of the tribe.

Most jobs centuries ago, were laborious and tedious, but were carried out with pride because they may have benefitted everyone. The connection with ancestors was one that stretched back through time to Divine Source. Your ancestors provide you with a very important link that is too valuable to lose or forget. It is time to reconnect with your past so that you can forge new sustainable links that will provide strength for you, your descendents, and future generations.

The heritage you retained is only a fraction of what it should be. It has been tattered, torn, and scattered to the four winds. You see, the Spirit never dies, and it cannot be destroyed. The essence of your ancestors can linger on throughout time and you can connect to them.

You are genetically linked forever to a group of individuals, which continues to expand through time and space. It is a small thing for you to reconnect to any dormant heritage if you choose to. Doing so, serves to bring you to a place of strength and stability.

The spiritual aspects of our lives represent an even deeper mystery. Those native to the continent appear to display the ability to connect spiritually to the unknown. Unfortunately, today many allow fear or the standards of others to impede their exploration of the unknown spiritual frontier. In years past that was not the case. The native people of that continent embraced the spiritual mysteries as part of their daily lives.

Travesty still ravages the continent through the progression of so-called higher civilizations. So many lives have been lost as well as land, and traditions. Countless numbers have been displaced and left in turmoil and or desolate like the land. This has compounded over centuries and has caused an insurmountable amount of devastation to the people that call this vast continent their Motherland. The sad part is that the people are to this day being moved about like pieces on a chessboard so that the land can be mined and stripped above and below ground.

Africa is considered to be the birthplace of man because the oldest skeletal remains are from that area. Although the exact location of man's birthplace is not known the anthological findings have revealed the general area through carbon dating. Because of that fact alone, I believe it is also the birthplace of spirituality as well. The spirit first took on the form of a human, plant, animal, or microorganism somewhere on this continent millions of years ago. Spiritual expression in mineral form was before that and will undoubtedly remain long afterwards.

Spirituality maybe the only true connection with the Divine. It is part of the lost heritage and may very well be the greatest lost. This loss is one of the main reasons an entire race is wandering the planet aimlessly. The Earth flourishes and many of the people flourish also, but for this race, the land is desolate and void wherever they happen to be. Some are attempting to fit in and find their way while many live like chameleons. Yet others appear to be running amuck and out of control.

Man has done this stripping, retraining and relocating experiment with different species of animals and has had a great deal of success. The problem with doing this experiment with people is that the brain factor comes into play. Humans have the ability to use reasoning and higher thinking. They have a brain with untapped potential and an immeasurable capacity for learning. This brain is a living organ that drives the human organism in ways that are unexpected. That means this living organism (human) has first hand, unlimited access to the super computer (the human brain) giving it the ability to adapt, at will.

This race is in a struggle to survive and recover from an ongoing genocidal attempt to wipe it from the face of the Earth. Maybe a genocidal attempt sounds harsh or over the top to you, but it is about the only way to explain some of the prior events that have occurred. You see, in the cases of animals, when all avenues of training have been exhausted and the animal continues to display unruly behavior, it is put down.

The treatment of some nonconformists can be compared to that of animals. With people, they are given a longer period of time locked up (imprisoned) than animals are. The biggest problem with that is in many cases some are treated far worse than animals. There are prison systems that are breeding grounds for the inhumane treatment against humans. After extensive stays in those types of environments the person's behavior is worse than before. He or she is unable to mentally function as a productive part of society and will oftentimes do something that would cause him or her to be returned to the penal system.

These things take place in many of the societies that label themselves as civilized. This type of thing did not occur in what many would call crude, savage, or uncivilized. Those societies seemed quite civilized to me because they were organized, had rules to govern behavior and daily living, and a system in place for dealing with issues that arose even nonconformists.

It is my belief that if this race would come into their true spiritual heritage, it would put them back on track and they would be more productive than destructive. A true spiritual balance is needed for them and for the world. The change that brings about balance must start at the source or prime position. That prime position would involve the location and people.

Of all the ethnicities on this planet, those of the darkest skin color seem to be the most hated. They are also the most feared. This race is looked at as the scum of the Earth. Other races seem to feel that the native people of Africa do not need or deserve land, respect, possessions, or other things. They are treated as if they only deserve meager handouts. Over seven countries invaded the African continent at different times and in different locations.

To this day many of the immigrants from those countries act as if they are entitled to the land and its natural resources (above and below the ground). They feel that it is okay to continue to take what they want and to just confine those native to a particular area or to just relocate them as they see fit in order to strip the land. The latest push is to preserve areas of the continent along with its wildlife. That of course is the ploy or cover story if you will. The fact is millions of acres of land are being sold to individuals and groups that are putting up these preserves and marketing them as Safaris. People are flocking to them as if they are the best thing since sliced bread. You can vacation on a Safari and stay at one of these so-called Preserves and entertain yourself by touring the areas of the Preserve to see the Natives in their natural habitat.

Some of the visitors get upset if the Natives try to sell their wares to them. They don't want to see Natives trying to sell them something they can buy in a Safari gift shop but they want to see them going about their daily lives so that they can have real African experiences with photos and video footage to take back and show their friends and associates. Some say it is an opportunity of a lifetime and the want their grandchildren to experience it. Now if that does not sound like a zoo for humans I do not know what does. How is it, in this day and age people that are native to that continent still cannot own the land?

These Safaris are really a type of African Bed & Breakfast that is being located on an African Preserve. The Preserve is just another name for Reservation. This type of Reservation is much like the Indian Reservations in America but with a few differences. There is an ongoing campaign of genocide concerning this race. Acts of the worst kind have been carried out and some are still being inflicted in an attempt to completely wipe this race off the face of the Earth.

Nowadays, many opportunities to advance are deliberately withheld from them but they are, in fact, their own worst enemy. Their low levels of education and lack of drive to pursue higher education in science, math, or professional fields, is crippling their advancement economically. Their broken family structure along with their desire and ability to connect with God poses the greatest threat to them and may very well be their biggest stumbling blocks. They fail to connect with God in the purest way, but act in accordance with the methods that others have given to them.

This action clouds the connection and hinders their ability to receive correct and useful information from God. They are forever trying to obtain that which they already have. To truly use their full potential or to progress in a successful manner they will need to go back to their true reality. To do this, they must reconnect with the true source of their being along with the truth of who they are and what makes them the individuals that they are and not some "cookie cutter" copy.

_____

Chapter 6

Roots

The roots of a plant give it life and sustain it throughout each year. Some plants appear to die, but the root system lies dormant underground until the time is right to re-emerge. A tree can lose leaves and branches and appear to be dead, but as long as its roots are healthy, it will spring forth new leaves and branches.

The root system of a plant or tree can also provide stability that helps it weather any storm or season. The roots spread as wide and as deep underground as the tree branches appear above ground in height and breadth. The root system is massive and complex because some of the roots feed nutrients to the tree, while others stabilize and anchor it.

Theoretically your ancestors are just like the root system of tree because they provide you with the same things. They feed you, anchor, and stabilize you both naturally and spiritually. Through them, you are provided the very basic genetic building blocks to sustain you so that you can contribute to the descendents that follow.

It is up to each individual to build upon that which was given to him or her. Whatever actions you take should add to that which was given to you. You should always strengthen that which you pass on to your descendants and the next generation. In this manner, you empower them to succeed and strengthen all that come after them.

Chapter 7

Scattering

Most people of African descent have no idea who they really are. Would I have you running around covered in grass skirts or loincloths? If that is your preference, yes! Do not get me wrong, I love the technology of this age and do not want to do without it, but grass skirts and loin cloths cover about as much as today's modern clothing covers. I do not believe a people should give up their entire heritage to be part of any civilized society.

To tell people that what they do culturally is wrong is in itself wrong. The right thing is to suggest a better, more efficient and effective way of doing things. In cases where a country or nation is conquered, implementing change brings less resistance than brute force. The same thing goes for the religious aspects of a society of people. History shows that religion is often used to condemn and enslave a people.

A conquering people will demonize the religion of the people that occupy the region. Their religious sites and objects are usually destroyed and the religion of the conquering people is then forced upon those native to the land. I have seen no God in history forcing its will upon the people except in some instances concerning mythology and that may have been a case of artistic licensing or embellishing. The people are given a choice by every god known to mankind. Humans feel they are serving God best if they force others to serve. Oftentimes, this means senseless killings are done in the name of their God, which only serves to feed a man's ego, to gain power, or wealth.

How diverse would a country be if it allowed its people to serve God in the manner which it was given in times past? You see, I cannot understand why the possibility of there being only one ultimate God with many different names never seems to enter the thoughts of some people. The constant debate that each religion has the true or ultimate God and all others are not really God is a large part of what keeps people at odds with each other. Of course if the purpose of keeping this going is to control and contain people through religion it is working quite well.

If you strip a person of everything, especially his or her God and you are able to be absolute in your efforts to control them. You can dictate and enforce certain laws and restrictions and you are able to contain them in a space, lifestyle, and condition. People are diverse and so are the languages, therefore, it is possible that each language would have a different name for God…and it be the same God. Just as different people have a different name for the same God, they have different ways of interacting with their God. It does not mean that it is wrong; it just means that it is different.

Most of the actions of those in charge were used to control and strip a race of its heritage. These were not just some "off the cuff" actions either but they were very calculated. This was a type of strategic conditioning that can be equated to mind control methods. They were coupled with torture techniques and they targeted fundamental core beliefs. Targeting the core beliefs in that fashion can have the greatest affect on a person's overall development. It becomes the fundamental makeup of the people being controlled.

Over time conditioning of that nature will affect not only the individual but also those generations that follow by passing along this learned information through a perpetual cycle. I believe those actions are the direct cause of a people being lost and scattered in the winds to the four corners of the Earth. Although some traditions appear useless to a current cause or even founded in myth they can still be quite valuable. They can help maintain order, pride, and morality that are needed in every society.

The heritage of a people and family is often passed through the cultural traditions and religion of a people. In centuries past very few things were written, but instead they were passed through teachings, songs, and tales. If traditions are stripped from the minds of a people they can never be passed on. The information is lost and with the passing of time so are the generations of people.

Chapter 8

The Great Rift

The Great Rift is the result of the collective actions of many nations coupled with time. It is an enormous divide that separates a people from its ancestors, history, heritage, and their ability to commune and walk with God. It came about because of the actions of civilized nations. These actions were carried out at many different times in history. They involved many different races of people and they took place for many different reasons.

If looked at for what it really accomplished, it would prove to be the biggest black mark on every nation that considered itself civilized. The Great Rift separated Mother from child, husband from wife, brother from sister, etc. The actions of the civilized nations perpetuated a break in many races. This break was so big and far reaching within one race that it sparked the genocide of the entire race.

Whether or not the intentions or actions of any of the civilized nations involved were to wipe out an entire race does not matter. Their actions set in motion a pure disregard for human life. Many of their actions can be viewed as blatant crimes against humanity.

The collective actions of others can have a big effect on an individual or a people but when coupled with time the effect can be more far-reaching and even greater. The passing of time can bring progress, advancement, and refinement. It can also cause deterioration, loss, erasure, and a dulling of senses. Time coupled with almost anything can exponentially affect many things in a positive or negative manner.

This humungous divide separates the people in this modern day from centuries of ancestors that came before them. It stripped the strong away from their country and all that they knew. It left the weak to fend for themselves and carry on. We are all connected by an invisible force. If we are able to utilize that force for good, it would be advantageous for all mankind.

If we are able to reconnect the modern race of people to the ancestral race, we could spark a restoration of a heritage. This is an ancestral heritage that was thought to be lost. It can be regained using our Sacred Journey techniques. You can change the tragedy of the Great Rift from a nightmarish reality into folkloric memory. People without a heritage are scattered wanderers with ties. They have no foundation that is tried, stable, or solid enough to build moral character or fortitude.

The foundation is shaky at best and cannot stand the tests that life throws at it. All that is built upon it will surely fall. Thus, the reality of this shows up everywhere as the many failed attempts at success. Through all of the struggles, only a small number of individuals have achieved a level of success that is noteworthy. Reconnecting the race with their ancestral heritage will help them regain a solid and diverse foundation. This foundation stretches back further than the origins of man. Their physical and spiritual actions are faint shadows of what they were before the Great Rift.

Chapter 9

Connecting with Source

The people of this race process a desire to connect with God appears to be driven by their struggles and situations but this is far from the truth. This is really part of a deeper survival mechanism that is encoded into their spiritual make up much like DNA and RNA is encoded into the very nucleus of the physical form. The spiritual realm calls and pulls at every fiber of their being.

The truth is one of the major travesties of the Great Rift. The generations have long sense forgotten how to truly commune and walk with God. They rely on the methods forced upon them by their captors. These methods are the combination of ideas, beliefs, myths, traditions, doctrines, and religious ideologies of others that have not been search out (logically or spiritually), but have been accepted as truths because they came from their captors.

The loss of the true spiritual communication with God has had a devastating affect on this race, but it has also caused hurt or harm to everyone and everything that occupies the Earth. I believe each race may have an assigned role while occupying this realm. This is an area in which they are able to excel in with minimal effort.

Through the act of conducting that role they as a people are able to advance and in turn they are able to help others. The assigned role of this race is that of a spiritual heartbeat. In fulfilling this role they are the priests that intercede and commune with God. These methods or ways have been abandoned to the point that it is hard for them to hear the voice of God. They run back and forth following the latest religious whim; looking to a man for answers and guidance. Some seek handouts; others make petitions and beg for assistance all the while never really communicating with God.

The benefits of restoring the true lines of communication with God are infinite. The benefits will surely help a people take their rightful place in the world, but these benefits will also help everyone and everything on the Earth. Remember this is really just a reawakening process to help reestablish what has been hidden or lying dormant in you.

PART II

PREPARATION FOR THE JOURNEY

Chapter 10

Tools

Items Needed

Cloth – *White, approximately 1 yard*
Locator *(purchased or made)*
Compass
Bottle of water - *unopened*
Clear glass or clear bowl
Food Color – *Blue or Green*
5 White Candles
5 Clear candleholders - *Foil can be used if performing journey outside*
Picture of Africa – *8 x 10 or larger*
Writing instrument - *pen, pencil, or marker*
Notepad/Journal
Dirt
Blank paper (unlined) - *few pieces*

Some of the items that will be used as tools can be purchased or constructed. It is your preference as to what you choose in all cases except when it comes to the cloth and the first set of candles. Those must be white because white is void of color. You do not want anything influencing the information that is making its way to you.

Locator

The locator is a simple pendulum. It is called a locator because it will help you locate places and find information. The locator can lead you, in other words, it does not just swing from side to side. You can purchase one or make one. It helps you connect quickly with that aspect of Divine Source within you. They can be fun and interesting to work with. If you are able to connect with Divine Source without it then by all means do so.

Using a locator tool can help cut down on the input from and of the ego. I like to pick all natural things or things that are close to the original state or content when it was in nature. Tips or points made from real minerals and not glass. Most handles are chains made from metal. I must say they tend to transmit energy currents more readily than cloth or string.

The metals themselves were mined or taken from the earth and have metaphysical properties as well. One of Einstein's theories state that in essence all things are related through a single thread which is energy. All that you see or experience is a different manifestation of energy. It is best to use items you like because they will help you maintain your focus and thereby yield the best results.

The type of pendulum you will be using has three parts. The tip or head is used to direct you, give you information, help locate things, move energy, etc. The body is used to allow the tip to freely swing or move. It has to be flexible to allow movement in any direction. The handle is attached to the end of the body that is opposite the tip or head. This is the part that you hold. It must not inhibit the movement of the body.

Cloth

You will need approximately 1 yard of a white silk, cotton, linen or other natural fiber. Do not use cloth made of nylon, polyester, permanent press, or synthetic material. We are going for the least amount of energetic interference. All of the materials will have received some type of chemical treatment but the natural fibers will be the best vehicles. You can leave the edges plain if you use pinking shears, otherwise you can fray them to look like fringes. You can also tidy the edges up with a hem by sewing, using iron-on tape, or even hot gluing.

You want to invest some of your time and energy into the items you use because this is an important journey on which you are about to embark. Keep the shape as a square or rectangle because it represents a foundation. This cloth is used throughout the entire Sacred Journey.

Compass

The compass will be used to locate the cardinal directions North, South, East, and West. It can be inexpensive but it is needed for use in each phase and area of the journey.

Water, container, food color

These items are only used in Phase Five but should be acquired and kept in the bundle until needed. The container can be small to medium in size but it must be clear and colorless. The food color can be blue or green. You will need a new unopened bottle of water to almost fill the container.

Candles, Holders, Foil

You will need five (5) white candles to start with and a clear candleholder for each one. If you are performing your Sacred Journey connection outside, you can opt to forego candleholders and use aluminum foil (as long as you can place them directly in the ground to steady them).

Once you connect to the different legs of your Sacred Journey, you may receive information concerning various colors and their uses. I suggest you wait until completing the journey once or wait until after the connection is made with the family before getting different colored candles. The tribal colors may differ slightly or completely from the family colors.

Picture or Map

You need an 8 x 10 copy of the entire African continent. It can be on regular paper because you will want to make marks on it. Besides, you will not be handling it with kid gloves and you may want to fold it later (picture quality paper does not fold well at all).

Dirt

If you perform this Sacred Journey connection indoors, you will need 1-2 pounds of dirt. If you are performing your journey outdoors and you have access to the ground or grass then this item is optional. It is used when making the connection with the Earth and then again when connecting to the African continent, however, making the connection when standing on the earth itself is much better.

I provide other suggestions that can be used as substitutes in the "Alternative Procedures" chapter. The connection phases involving dirt are extremely important to the success of your journey and they must be done.

Blank Paper

The blank pieces of paper will be used to program the Locator and for making Suggestion cards when finding answers.

Miscellaneous

Other items that are useful to have are a notepad or journal, a writing instrument and a few pieces of blank paper. You need notepad, journal, and writing instrument for the obvious reasons. You may want to mark locations on the picture or you may want to jot down information, descriptions, or pictures you receive. The universal or cosmic language is pictures so you may see pictures and you can draw what you see. You do not need to be an artist, but when making a picture or sketch, you want to put as much detail as you are able to, along with notes about it.

Cuneiform and hieroglyphics are the earliest recorded forms of written language. They were used to communicate using basic, crude pictorial shapes. Your drawings can also provide good conversation pieces, with others that have taken this journey. They can be compared and merged with other family members to form a broader understanding and a database of information pertaining to your ancestral heritage. They can be compilations of family information to be passed on to future generations because it is part of their heritage as well.

Chapter 11

Gathering Tools

You want to make sure the items you gather for this project are new and have not been used for another purpose.

<u>Cloth</u>

The cloth is prepared by manipulating the edges. You can both fold the edges to create a clean look then secure them by sewing (hand or machine) or using an iron-on bonding tape. The other options are to use a type of stop fray along the edges or create a fringed border by removing piece of thread to create frayed edges. Make sure you do not put any markings or color on it because it needs to remain colorless. This cloth will be used through the entire Sacred Journey.

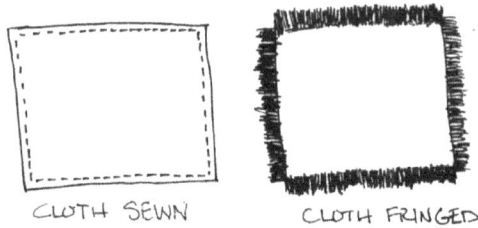

CLOTH SEWN   CLOTH FRINGED

It will be used as a bag, sack, or carryall bundle. All items will be placed on top of the cloth in the center. Gather two opposite corners upwards towards the center and tie once.

1ST TIE
OPPOSITE SIDES

2ND TIE
SECOND OPPOSING SIDES

Gather the remaining two opposite corners in the same manner and tie once. Taking a loose end from each of the previous knots, tie the bundle again.

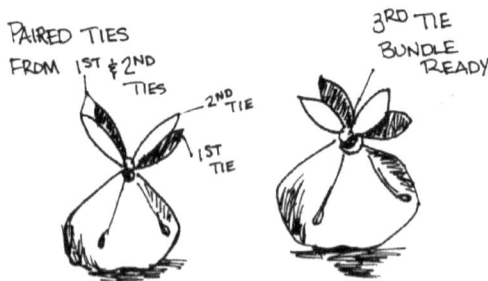

PAIRED TIES FROM 1ST & 2ND TIES
2ND TIE
1ST TIE

3RD TIE
BUNDLE READY

Make sure to tie each part once not twice so that the bundle will untie easily. Using the cloth in this manner allows you to move and transport all items at once. You want to keep all items tied in the cloth when they are not being used.

Picture

You will need an 8 x 10 picture of the African continent. You can get a larger size if you so desire. You can make a copy of the one in the Sacred Journey book if you like. It can be in color or black and white. It also folds better if it is copied on regular paper versus photo paper. You will use this for the entire Sacred Journey. This picture will become your ancestral map. It will become your treasured possession to show you the places of your ancestors.

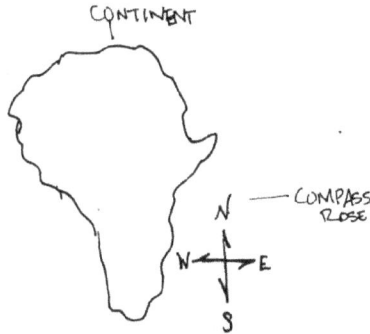

Make sure it is a picture of the African continent and not a world map. Place a simple compass rose on it to transform it into a map. This helps to orient you when traveling around the continent. As you get information, you can, in turn, place marks on the map.

Dirt

Get approximately 1-2 lbs of dirt and place it in a Ziploc bag. You will need to use this dirt for the first two legs of your Sacred Journey. You are free to use it afterwards if you like. It is best that you gather this from the earth. Potting soil mixtures may contain debris. However, you may use fill dirt or other such items sold in stores if it does not contain the debris.

***You only need to get dirt if you cannot perform your Sacred Journey outside on the ground with full access to the ground itself and not concrete or other surfaces. It needs to be dirt – <u>earth</u>.

Candles & Holders

Disclaimer & Safety Note:
Take extra precautions when using candles and fire as serious damage can occur. Never leave burning candles unattended. Always use fireproof containers for burning candles because other types of containers can melt or break. Keep burning candles and open flames clear of flammable materials.

Take 5 white candles and put them on the cloth. You can place them in a sandwich bag if you like to prevent the wax from rubbing onto the other items; you will prepare them for use later. Votive candles work best because they are wider and more stable than stick candles.

You want to get 5 clear glass holders or 5 white ceramic holders. Either one is fine, as long as they are free from color and unnecessary markings. You want to sandwich white paper between each or wrap them in white paper to keep them from breaking. Place them in the center of your cloth as well. The candles will light your way and serve as beacons of light for your ancestors to find you. See Preparing Candles chapter for important information concerning candles.

Alternative candleholder:

You can use aluminum foil to hold candles when conducting your connection outside. The idea is to use the ground to secure the candles in place.

- Cut a nice-sized square to fit your candle size. (Votives work well)
- Place candle in the center of the square.
- Wrap the aluminum foil upwards around entire candle.
- Crumple the edges of the aluminum foil around the entire candle, thereby creating a makeshift bowl.
- Dig a slight hole for the candle to sit in.

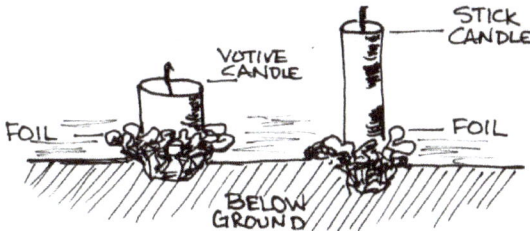

Locator

If you choose to purchase one from the store it will already be assembled. Select one with a head or tip made of Quartz Crystal or Hypersthene. Once you get it home place it in a sandwich bag and put it on the center of the cloth you will work with it later.

This item will be used to show you where things and people were located. It can show the places people traveled to and the routes they took to get there. See Programming Locator chapter to prepare it for use. After you discover your family colors, you can make or acquire a cloth bag or fabric in that color to keep your Locator in when carrying or storing it in your bundle.

Alternative Locator:

Use this method if you cannot or do not want to purchase a ready-made pendulum. You will assemble your locator out of found items as stated in below labeled. Once you have assembled your locator, place it inside a sandwich bag, and put it on the center of the cloth. This will work just like a store bought pendulum.

Head/Tip
Rock
Crystal
Acorn
Twig

Body
String
Chain
Cord
Vine
Palm tree fronds (shredded thinly in strips)

The final length of the body should be no less than 6 inches long. You will need a few inches to tie around the tip and handle material. The size of them will be the determining factor.

Handle
Metal ring or loop
Bead

You only need one of each of the items listed above but you may choose to construct more Locators using the different items suggested.

Constructing the Locator

Tie the string around the item you will use as the tip or head. Secure the other end to the item you will use as the handle. It is ready to use. An alternative method would be to drill a hole in the item you will use as a tip. Thread the handle material through the hole. Adjust the handle material so that it is an even length on both sides. Tie the two ends together using the newly tied portion as the handle.

If the head has a sharp point, as the case with an arrowhead, it can pinpoint locations better than a wide point can. A twig from a tree can be shaped to a point by whittling it with a knife or blade or by using an abrasive file, concrete surface, or sandpaper.

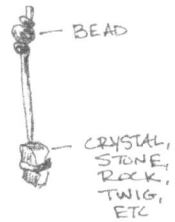

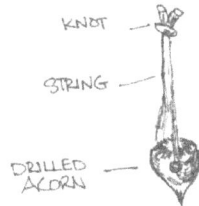

BEAD

CRYSTAL,
STONE,
ROCK,
TWIG,
ETC

KNOT

STRING

DRILLED
ACORN

Miscellaneous Items

Other items that you will need because they will be useful to have: pen/marker, notepad/journal, lighter, and a compass.

Chapter 12

Preparing Candles

The candles serve two major purposes. They are used to light your path while on your Sacred Journey and act as a beacon. This beacon allows those in your ancestral past to follow the light to you. The candles are especially good to use during the actual connection times. Everything leaves an invisible print that can last through the ages. This light will be as the stars that appear in the night sky. Although we can see them they are said to have burned out years or even centuries ago…but yet we see them.

Using the candles is optional after you have made the initial connections for each area. It is up to you if and how to use them after the initial connections. Establish certain ground rules for their use up front and try to stick with them to avoid confusion. For instance, you may want to use them when making an initial connection to a particular ancestor. You can then connect with that ancestor again without using a candle. Some feel the lighted candle adds to the connection and therefore they always use a candle. Others tell ancestors that they will use a candle as a signal for them to come close, establish a connection, and share information. Candles are especially good to use when you want access to information concerning an event or gathering.

The first five candles you use will not last for the entire journey unless you are using Seven-Day candles. I do not recommend using those unless you note which candle represents you and you are able to keep that straight. It is important that you do not use the other candles to represent yourself. Everything has its own distinct vibration. Once you dedicate an object for a particular purpose only use it for that purpose as to avoid any confusion.

You can carve your name on a candle or its container but no colored markings are allowed. The candle that represents you is very important so it is best to get a few and prepare them in advance. The candle that represents you will be used in every session so you may need to have more than one candle on hand during the course of your journey. When one candle burns out completely then you will have another readily available.

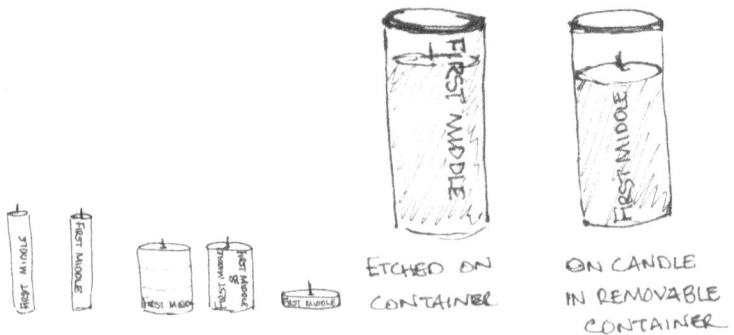

ETCHED ON CONTAINER

ON CANDLE IN REMOVABLE CONTAINER

The five candles used for the first two connection phases must be white (void of color). This is to minimize interference associated with color or things that color can attract. The candles used for the initial connection to the ancestral tribe and family must also be white as well. The candles you use for further interaction with the tribe and family can be in the appropriate colors for them.

This information will come to you as you interact with your ancestors and it can be used for later encounters and meetings.

In order to effectively use candles for your Sacred Journey you will need to prepare them. Preparing any object involves cleaning and programming it for a specific purpose. Cleaning means removing any adverse energy vibrations of others the object has come in contact with. Programming it means telling it what you intend to use it for and energizing it for that purpose. You will do this for each new candle that you use. The only exception to this is when you purchase especially prepared objects and kits.

Cleaning Method 1

1. Take the candle in your hand under the flow of running water (allow water to wash over the entire surface of the candle.
2. Say aloud, "This candle is being cleaned and cleared of any adverse vibrations that may have attached themselves to it."
3. Dry the candle off.

Cleaning Method 2

1. Take the candle in your hand and fully submerge it in a running stream of water or in ocean waves.
2. Say aloud, "This candle is being cleaned and cleared of any adverse vibrations that may have attached themselves to it."
3. Dry the candle off.

Cleaning Method 3

1. Place the candle in a container of sea salt allowing the salt to fully cover the candle. Some people like to make a declaration at this point such as, "Cleanse this candle of all adverse energies." A declaration is not necessary because the

salt will naturally cleanse the item. You can however state it if you like.

2. Leave in sea salt for at least 15 minutes.
3. Remove and use

Chapter 13

Programming Candles

It is necessary to adjust the energy of the candles that you will use for your Sacred Journey. Adjusting the energy changes them from being ordinary candles and makes them special candles. This change causes them to take a state of being created for a specific purpose instead of a general purpose. Whenever one of these candles burn completely out, use the steps in this chapter to prepare more. You can prepare a few in advance if you like or you can wait until you need another one.

Programming Candles

Hold the candle in both hands and state the purpose for its use. Make this statement or something similar to this:

"I empower you for the purpose of helping me make connections along my Sacred Journey. You will light my sacred space throughout this journey and serve as a shining beacon for my ancestors to find me."

Programming Personal Candle

When programming the candle that represents you, follow this two-step process to personalize and empower it. This will adjust the vibrations of the candle for your use.

Step One

Carve your name on the candle to personalize it. Do not use anything that will leave color markings on the candle.

This can be done using a pen, stylus, or other sharp object to engrave your name on it. You only want to use your first and middle name on the candle for this process. There are several reasons for not using the last name. The main reason for that is because you are connecting to your true ancestral past and your family's name is not known at this time. This is your past before the "Great Rift."

Your name must be written on the surface of the candle (preferably on the side or body of the candle).

If the only exposed surface of the candle is the top then you must also write your name somewhere on the container the candle is in. Electric or battery operated engravers work well for etching on the glass surface. If you do not have that then keep it separated from the others. Remember not to use any color on the white candles or holders.

If using a candle that can be removed from its container then write your names on the sides. Write your name in a direction from top to bottom or bottom to top. If the candle is large enough you can write around the circumference within the bottom 1/3 portion.

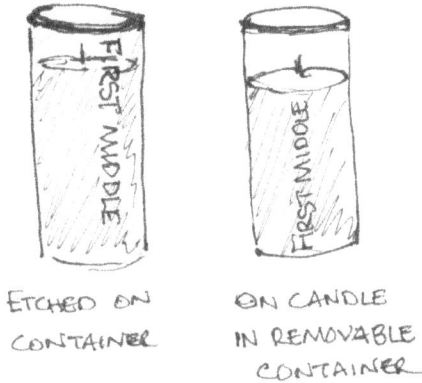

ETCHED ON CONTAINER

ON CANDLE IN REMOVABLE CONTAINER

If it is a tea light candle then you would remove it, write your name on it, and then replace it.

The personalized candle is extremely important and is easier to keep track of when partnering with others during a Sacred Journey.

Step Two

In this step you will empower the candle to become an extension of you. Hold the candle in both hands once you have written your name on it. Now state the purpose. Make this statement or one similar to it.

"I empower this candle for the purpose of representing me when I make connections and move along my Sacred Journey. This candle with my name on it will light my path through the ages. It will serve as a shining beacon of light for my ancestors to find me and recognize me."

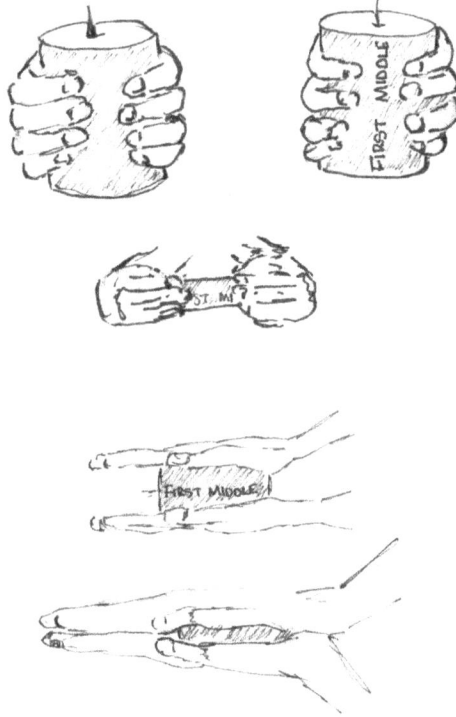

You can ask God, Angels, or others to help empower these objects for your purpose. That is it. You can now place the candles inside your bundle and use it later.

Chapter 14

Programming Locator

Programming the Locator allows you the opportunity to establish a basic means of communication between you and the Locator. This means there is a common ground in place when seeking answers. Many times the clutter and flow of thoughts clouds the path and the seeker finds it hard and sometimes impossible to receive answers. Anxiety will also prevent or stand in your way and pose obstacles. Anxiety has a way of rapidly fueling the flow of thoughts with negativity and doubt. This particular type of thought will almost always cause a huge break in communication between you and the Locator.

Programming a Locator can be done at anytime. The optimal time is when you first acquire a Locator or after you have spent some time with it but never just before you <u>need</u> to use it. Most physical items have been in contact with others, even if it was only brief encounters. You will need to allow the Locator time to take on your vibrations. In other words, it will need to get rid of anyone else's vibrations and be influence only by you. This is done best by bathing it in your vibrations. You can do this by keeping it near you or on your person.

Keep it near you because it really is an extension of the Divine within you. You can place it under your pillow, in your pocket or purse; next to the chair you occupy the most, etc. Once you have kept it near you for several days or nights, you are ready to proceed with verbal commands. These are really just possible answers that the Locator will display. You will tell the Locator to show you the movement it will make for a specific answer. Later, when you ask it a question, it will display the movement for you.

The movements and corresponding answers stated here are basic. You are at liberty to make your own. The basic answers are: YES, NO, MAYBE SO (YES), & MAYBE NOT (NO). Some people lean towards UNDECIDED. To me, an undecided is still a "maybe." I find that, even when people say maybe or undecided, they are usually leaning towards yes or no. With that stated, we can move on to the actual programming for answers.

You will need three (3) pieces of plain, unlined, and unmarked paper approximately 4" x 5" in size. This can be the result of folding a regular sheet of copy paper in half, once horizontally and once vertically. Cut or tear along the folds and you will have four pieces of paper. Use one single piece at a time. I do not write on them as a stack.

You can tell the Locator which movement you want it to make in order to represent a specific answer or you can let it show you on its own. I prefer the latter, since the Locator is in touch with the Divine part of Source dwelling within me. I feel it will always show me what is best.

Movements

The Locator can make several movements. The most frequent movements a Locator make are: back and forth, side to side, diagonal, left, right, circular (clockwise, counter clockwise), motionless and shaking. The left or right of the diagonal is judged by the leading edge of the swing or the part that is furthest away from you.

Some people use the circular movement to indicate a maybe answer, but I use the diagonal movement for that. The Locator will use the circular movement for more elaborate answers or to adjust energy. To avoid any confusion when seeking answers, it is best to reserve that movement for later uses. Therefore, for now, we will focus on gaining answers using the vertical, horizontal, diagonal. We will use the circular movement to adjust the energy so that we can gain access to information a little easier.

When a Locator stands still, it is usually because the user does not believe it will move or that it can be useful in obtaining information. When a Locator shakes, it is displaying the nervousness, anxiety, or fear of the user. When a Locator displays a combination of movements or refuses to move, it can be trying to keep up with the thoughts or emotions of the user. The movement many new users display is a slight swing, then shaking.

You must always remain calm and in control of your thoughts when using a Locator. You can use meditation to calm yourself or just use happy thoughts. The idea is to maintain stress free contact with the pendulum. Once you get use to the idea of it being able to move when you ask it questions you will not need to do anything but pick it up and ask away.

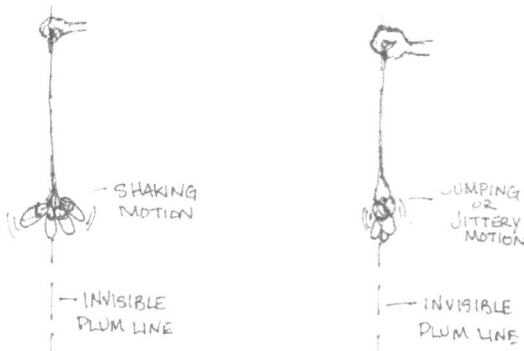

YES & NO

- Place one piece of paper in front of you and draw a good-sized plus sign in the middle of it.
- Set everything else off to the side.
- Take the Locator in your dominant hand (the hand you use for writing). Holding it by the handle (using three fingers), allow it to hang directly over the center of the plus sign.
- Calm your being by taking several deep breaths.
- Clear your mind of thoughts.
- State: "Show me YES" – This can be a verbal or mental statement. Those new to this should state everything verbally. Doing so allows you to better see how the Locator responds and it also helps you control your thoughts when working with a Locator.
- Allow the Locator to swing while remaining calm.
- Keep your voice calm, but assertive and repeat the command if necessary.

The Locator will swing along the vertical or horizontal line that you have drawn. This will be the movement to represent a 'YES' answer.

- Grab the point in your other hand.
- Say, "Thank you."
- Place the Locator to the side or in your lap.
- Write "YES" at both ends of the line that represent a 'YES' answer.
- Write 'NO' at both ends of the other line.
- Repeat the steps from the beginning, but use the same plus sign paper that is in front of you. This time, you will tell the Locator to show you 'NO'. It should swing along the line marked NO.

YES

NO

YES —————— YES

NO ——————— No

NO

YES

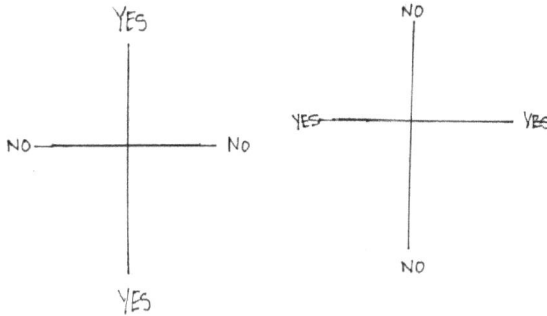

This is just a formality, but it is important. Once it swings along the direction of the line marked 'NO', you can stop it as before and say thank you. Now you may feel that it is crazy to be talking to an inanimate object and saying thank you to it, but that is not the case. You are using the Locator as a tool to gain access to information and answers. These answers and information are within the mind of Divine Source. Once Divine Source, or any other being, releases information to you through any means, you should say thank you. It is the polite and normal thing to do; especially, if you would like their assistance again in the future.

MAYBE YES & MAYBE NO

You will do similar steps for MAYBE as you did for YES & NO, With MAYBE you will be substituting an 'X' the place of a plus signs.

- Place one piece of paper in front of you and draw a good-sized "X" in the middle of it.
- Set everything else off to the side.
- Take the Locator in your dominant hand. Holding it by the handle (using three fingers), allow it to hang directly over the center of the "X".
- Calm your being by taking several deep breaths.

- Clear your mind of thoughts except the statement you direct to the Locator.
- State: Show me MAYBE YES – This can be a verbal or mental statement. Those new to this should state everything verbally. Doing so allows you to better see how the Locator responds and it also helps you control your thoughts when working with a Locator.
- Allow the Locator to swing while remaining calm.
- Keep your voice calm, but assertive and repeat the command if necessary.

The Locator will swing along the diagonal line that you have drawn. This will be the movement to represent a MAYBE YES answer.

- Grab the point of the Locator in your other hand.
- Say, "Thank you."
- Place the Locator to the side or in your lap.
- Write MAYBE YES at both ends of the line that represent a YES answer.
- Write MAYBE NO at both ends of the other line.
- Repeat the steps from the beginning, but use the same paper that is in front of you. This time, you will tell the Locator to show you MAYBE NO.

It should swing along the correct diagonal line. Once it swings along the direction of the line marked 'MAYBE NO', you can stop it as before and say thank you.

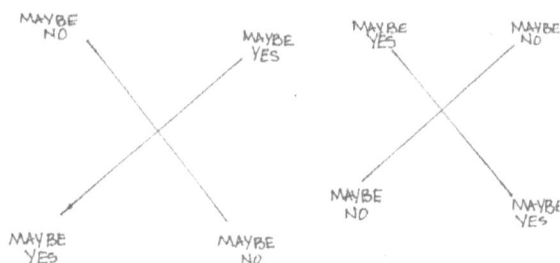

Adjusting Energy or Vibrations

When you adjust the energy of something, you are merely interacting in a manner that will make adjustments to the vibrations. This can be done for any number of reasons. The majority of the time it is done to help bring about a state of wellness to an individual. It is also done to help individuals reach higher levels of consciousness (enlightenment, high thoughts).

I have found that this is an excellent way to create an ideal environment for a meeting or seminar. Therefore, I offer the information here to help create the ideal conditions for you to work in when seeking answers along your Sacred Journey.

CLOCKWISE & COUNTER CLOCKWISE

- Place one piece of paper in front of you and draw a good-sized circle in the middle of it.
- Set everything else off to the side.
- Take the Locator in your dominant hand.
- Holding it by the handle (using three fingers), allow it to hang in a position directly in the center of the circle.
- Calm your being by taking several deep breaths.
- Clear your mind of thoughts.
- State: "Show me CLOCKWISE" – This can be a verbal or mental statement. Those new to this should state everything verbally. Doing so allows you to better see how the Locator responds and it also helps you control your thoughts when working with a Locator.
- Allow the Locator to swing while remaining calm.
- Keep you voice calm, but assertive and repeat the command if necessary.

The Locator will swing in a clockwise manner.

- Grab the point in your other hand.

- Say "Thank you."
- Repeat the steps from the beginning, but use the same circle that is in front of you. This time, you will tell the Locator to show you COUNTER CLOCKWISE.

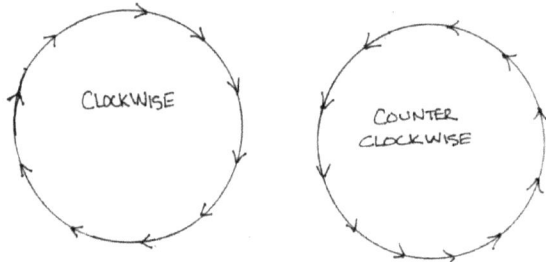

Keep in mind that these movements will help create good working conditions. The Locator may move in either or both directions to get the job done. If you see the movement now, you will avoid being shocked or surprised by a new movement later.

Advanced Programming

Below is what a normal Selection Card would look like. After working with a Locator for a bit you will not need to use a Selection Card. Practice using this type of Selection Card as you would when you first programmed the Locator. The differences will be in the commands and the addition of the command STOP.

- Place the completed Selection Card in front of you.
- Set everything else off to the side.
- Take the Locator in your dominant hand.
- Holding it by the handle (using three fingers), allow it to hang directly over the center.
- Calm your being by taking several deep breaths.
- Clear your mind of thoughts except the statement you direct to the Locator.
- State: YES.

- Allow the Locator to swing while remaining calm.
- Keep you voice calm, but assertive and repeat the command if you need to.

The Locator will swing along the vertical or horizontal line labeled YES.

- Now state the word: STOP. Notice the swinging motion as it will begin to slow down and stop in the original position. If it does not, remain calm and firmly state the word STOP again. It should then stop.
- Say, "Thank you."
- Repeat the same steps for the NO and MAYBE commands

Sometimes when programming or asking the Locator for help in finding information, you may find it quite advantageous to visualize or picture what you are asking about in your mind. Remember pictures are a universal language that transcends regular languages.

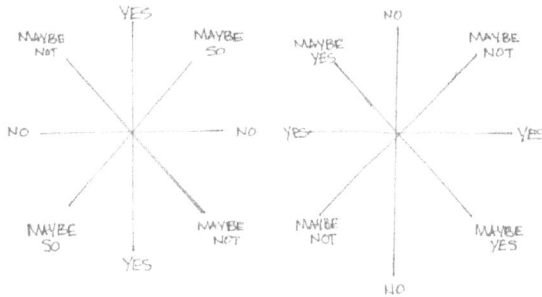

Now that the programming part is complete, the Locator can be used when you are ready. You can try it out with test questions if you would like. Remember, that your thoughts move extremely quickly, so you must not allow them to dart from question to question because the Locator will try to keep up with the changing of your thoughts. You want to remain calm and pleasant so that you are not interfering with the information that is being sent to you.

***It is important to always keep the Locator with you or in your bundle of items you use for your Sacred Journey.

Chapter 15

Dedication and Petitioning

Most of the preliminary things have been done. Next, you will need to dedicate the items that you will be using. You should have placed all of your items on the cloth. These items should be kept together in the cloth for the duration of your journey; the exception being the notepad or journal.

You want to keep that with you in case information comes to you throughout the day. Otherwise, you can keep it in the cloth with the other items. There is nothing hard or fancy that needs to be done. You must keep or hold your purpose in your mind and intend to do whatever is within your power to hold true to the use of the items for a specific reason.

With the items set before you in the center of the cloth, you will make a declaration for the intended use of the items, along with a petition for assistance to accomplish your Sacred Journey. You want to be certain and sincere. Nothing is worse than asking someone for help and you do not know what you need him or her to do. The same goes for saying that you will do one thing but do another, constantly changing your mind about a matter or acting as if you are not sure what you really want to do.

You should take the time to make up your mind about what you are going to do and when and where you will do it. As for the what, that has already been decided. You can just follow the directions given in this book. You must decide when you will start your Sacred Journey and where you conduct each leg of the journey.

The first two legs should be done outside, while you are standing on the ground. It can be bare ground (dirt) or grass. It should not be on asphalt, concrete or other surfaces. If you cannot place your feet on the ground, then you must gather dirt to use as stated in the chapter on Tools. For instance, you have a patio, but no bare or grassy ground. You can do it on the patio, using the dirt that you gathered.

When doing any part of your journey, you want to do it in a place and at a time that you will not be rushed or made to feel uncomfortable. In other words, you may need to be completely alone. The exception to this is if you and another person decided to partner up. I will give more information concerning that in the Alternative chapter.

Once you have a good idea where and when, you can proceed to the dedication and petitioning. Nothing is absolute and set in stone and things occur that cause us to make adjustments. Therefore, if you have to change something later, that is okay, but even then, be decisive.

Dedication

Use the script provided or something very similar. You are going to dedicate the entire bundle at once. It can be open or closed. Make contact with it during your dedication statement. Your contact can be touching it with a finger or hand(s).

"I dedicate these items that lie before me to the purpose of helping me complete my Sacred Journey that will connect me to my ancestors and restore to me my full and rightful heritage that will help me successfully move through this life."

Make sure that you only use the items for the intended purpose. Tie the cloth by pulling two diagonal corners upwards towards the center and tying it once. Take the other two diagonal corners and loosely tie them twice. Make sure the last two are tied loosely because you will need to use the bundled contents.

Petition

Personalize this script by using the names of your God, helpers, angels, etc. You also want to insert your name or references to yourself when appropriate. Make the petition plain, simple, and short. If you need to plead with someone for them to help you, then they really do not want to assist you and you are better off looking elsewhere for assistance.

"I, __your name__ ask __the entities that you seek assistance from__ to assist me in quickly and successfully completing this Sacred Journey that will reconnect me with my ancestors and restore to me my true and rightful heritage that will help me successfully travel through this life. Thank you for your assistance with this matter."

The following information being presented is important to the success of your Sacred Journey. I cannot emphasize its importance enough and therefore I will tell you now that this step should not be overlooked. Before you begin any of the phases of your Sacred Journey you will need to do an odd thing with your bundle of supplies. It is a necessary step, so please do not neglect it.

After you have prepared, bundled, and dedicated all of the items you will use for your journey find a spot in your yard, bury the bundle in the ground mark the spot, and walk away. Leave it buried for at least 15 minutes. Maintain the thought of discovering a large buried treasure when retrieving your bundle.

If you do not have access to a yard to do that then you will need to go to a park or other area and place the bundle on the ground or grass. You can set it beside you, under a park bench and read a book while it is sitting on the ground for at least 30 minutes. The bundle is interacting with the vibrations of the Earth so this is a step that is needed before you use the items.

After you have completed all of the above actions place your bundle of tools in a place that it will not be disturbed by others, but it will be near you. If you can find such a place, put it where others will not touch, disturb, or hang over it. From time to time, get it from its stored place and keep it near you. You can place it near you on a table, under your chair or bed, in your lap or on the floor next to you. You spend time near it so that it gets your vibrations on it.

PART III

THE SACRED JOURNEY

Chapter 16

Creating the
Sacred Journey Space

This is a beautiful, powerful, and moving experience. My preference for reestablishing an ancestral connection is outside at night. I have no preference as to the size of the setup. The choice is yours and ultimately such factors as living area, location, access to areas and privacy would determine which methods you would use. You can try both, the indoor and outdoor methods, if you would like. Our aim is to make the best connection possible to bring about the best results. This may mean using whichever method that will allow you to be relaxed, receptive, and comfortable.

If performed at night, the majority of daily activities in the area have stopped. The atmospheric energy has also changed to a calmer, more fluid and less aggressive nature. The energy from people will have changed as well. All of these changes provide for less interference, which allows you to connect easier and allows information to flow more smoothly. Whether it is performed at night or during the day, the experience is quite moving and restorative.

The entire journey can be performed indoors or outdoors. I have found the overall experience to be more enriching when conducted outside. The outdoor environment allows for more freedom of movement because it is less confining. It allows for energy to move more freely. The energy is moving across time, space, and dimensions. My suggestions on choosing the size of the set up depends upon the weather and the number of ancestors you are connecting with. If you are connecting with a family, group, or an entire tribe, use a larger size. If you are connecting to 1-3 individuals then go with a smaller size.

You are able to see and experience tribal meetings, events, gatherings, traditions, etc and will be able to distinguish what is going on through observation and through asking questions. The interaction of the tribe can also be assessed as well. Hunting parties and coming of age parties and initiations, are just a few of the things you can access.

Preparations for marriage, child bearing, child rearing, and behavior patterns are seemingly encoded in us through our ancestry but are part of what is taught and can be accessed. Invisible and lost as they may be, they continue to shape our actions, along with our present environment. We move through life as puppets, being directed by invisible strings. Making choices based on information passed along an invisible broken line. Because the line is broken we miss out on what falls through the gaps.

We want to use the techniques presented to step back along the spiritual path through time and dimension in order to get the information that will mend the breaks, tears, and rips, thereby causing a restoration to take place. No longer will we be disjointed and at odds, confused or against one another. We can be at a place of wholeness and unite one with another as in past ages.

Candle Setup

You will use five candles to accomplish the initial connection of each phase. Once the initial connection with a particular leg of your journey has been established you can then use one candle (the one that represents you) or none at all. Please see "Preparing Tools Chapter" for more details.

In the basic setup four candles are always set in the shape of a square and one candle is always placed inside of the square. After the initial connection phase with an ancestor you can then use only one candle if you choose to continue using candles. The candles are to remain lit as you move through the area of the journey.

For instance, you begin your Sacred Journey by connecting to the Earth. You will light the candles and keep them lit until that session is complete. This could be anywhere from a few minutes to hours. Once it is over, snuff out the candles, and use them for the next phase and area of the journey. You want to snuff out the candle's flame instead of blowing it out. Blowing out a candle tends to make the statement that you are finished with it.

This using of candles is done each time you embark on an area of your Sacred Journey. Ideally Phases and travel through the various contact areas are set up and conducted outside on the ground. However, all can be conducted indoors if needed. See Alternate Procedures for variations.

1. Put the Locator in your pocket or on your person
2. Determine the cardinal direction (North, South, East, West) you are going to use, then locate it using the compass.
3. Place your four candles in position. This means each should be in a cardinal direction. The candles are spaced approximately two arm lengths apart by holding your arms up and outward while standing in the middle. Make the space smaller only if you do not have much room.

Measuring out the Area

The fifth candle represents you and is placed in position once you are in place within the space of the candles.

C1-C5 CANDLES
M - MAP
CH - CHAIR (optional)

Sacred Space

Your Sacred Journey space has been created and now you can follow the directions for the phase and area you intend to travel through. If conducting the phases and travels of your Sacred Journey indoors or in an area where no earth is present see the Alternative Procedures chapter.

Chapter 17

Making the Connections

All things appear to die or end, to exist, and return to the Earth in one form or another. Some things are consumed by others, but, eventually, it all is reconnected to the Earth. The Earth is the one big connection we all have to this physical realm. We will therefore, use it to "Bridge the Gap." The Earth is like a time capsule. We can use it to reconnect with what is on it or what is in it.

The information you glean, will help to give you greater insight as to who you are and where you come from. It may also help you decide where you are going. You can also use this information to help you when forming habits, setting goals (long or short) and when choosing a mate or companionship. If you focus on connecting with the Earth to make the reconnection with your ancestors, then knowing the exact locations that they lived in will not matter.

You can make several different types of connections after doing the initial connection phase. You are able to make individual connections to specific relatives as far back in time as you would like. It may be that you only want to reconnect with ancestors belonging to a specific generation. You can choose either paternal ancestors, maternal ancestors or both. You are also able to connect with an ancestral community as a whole. You are not trying to communicate with those that have transitioned from this realm (that can be found in a different forum).

You are reconnecting with the essence of what was lost. This is what your ancestors would have graciously bestowed upon you had the lineage not been ripped apart. This is part of your heritage, it is your birthright. Carrying out this action, will help to create the essence of wholeness within you.

Aside from the objects you have gathered, you will need to possess a mental readiness. If you are not prepared mentally, then you will reject the knowledge and information that comes to you. If you reject the knowledge and information, then taking the journey would be a waste of time.

In order to make any connections along your journey, you must not only be receptive but you must remain receptive, open, focused, and centered. Some find it useful to visualize using the information that is received along the way. The information you receive will be different. You may tend to reject it based on biases learned on this side of the "Great Rift."

Receive all information and make note of it in your journal or note pad. It can be like receiving or flipping over pieces of a puzzle. You do not get the full picture at once, but each piece has its place and when put in its proper place, it will give a whole picture. Each piece is needed in order to bring a complete and useful foundation to you. Therefore, you must maintain receptiveness at all times.

You must also be able to focus your thoughts and do not allow them to wander off onto other subject matters. You want to keep to the intended purpose of your Sacred Journey. To center yourself will mean to calm your entire being. Do not allow anxiety or stress to creep in. Shed the cares of the day so that you are free to connect and associate with your ancestors. This is why it is important to plan the time and day you will make any connection. You want to be uninterrupted and free from daily cares.

You can use various things to help you meditate (focus), and make connections. Some use animals, trees, plants, and music. The most popular thing used in meditation music coupled with nature, tribal, birds, ocean, and animal sounds. Meditating on these things may cause you to daydream which is good.

You want to make notations concerning your daydreams also, because the information you see, hear, or sense can be useful later. The more you make connections along your Sacred Journey, the easier it will be for you to connect at will. Use the information obtained from one area to help connect to the next area. It acts like a focusing device.

Chapter 18

Journeying Through Time and Space

You will utilize five major phases that will open the five important areas involved in your Sacred Journey. Each one is just as important as the one that precedes it. Alone, each is significant, but together they lay a foundation that will allow you to regain what has been lost to your family for centuries. Each will have an enormous impact on putting you in direct contact with your true heritage.

You are not trying to return to the jungle, to a barren land, or to old ways. You are not trying to return to a state that some have classified as savage (before modernization and advancements in science and technology). You are merely reclaiming a foundational part of yourself that will empower and enable you to move forward in a more productive manner.

Your movement along your Sacred Journey will be from a wide aspect to a narrow one. You will move from the Earth, to a continent, to a tribe, then to a family. There are three ways to travel along your Sacred Journey. One way is that you can connect then quickly move along the major areas; then later you can go back through each to gain greater details. The second way to move along your Sacred Journey is to connect to each major area and thoroughly explore each before moving to the next phase. The third way involves a combination of the two previously stated methods. There is a lot of information in each of these areas and I believe using the third method gives you the most flexibility.

Connect to an area using a phase, gather a few tidbits of information, and explore points of interest more in-depth then move on to the next area. Once you have connected to each area of the journey and receive enough information to fill in some of the historical gaps or information for your map, you can then revisit each major area for more detailed information about briefly noted things.

General

It is important to use the same location to make revisits when reconnecting to ancestors or tribesmen. Your orientation for each will be to the Cardinal North, South, East, or West. You can try facing each direction to see which orientation allows you to connect and receive information easier. North and East directions are often used for navigation purposes to help find bearings when lost or traveling. The Egyptians, Israelites, and Ancients use the East for various reasons. One very important reason was that it is the direction in which the Sun rises at the beginning of each new day.

Most people face or orient themselves to the Cardinal West when looking for hidden information or mysteries. This information may be hidden by time, but it has occurred and lies in your past so any orientation can be used. Placing a compass rose on the map of the continent serves its purpose no matter which direction you use. Experiment at first by standing in different directions and positions to see which direction feels better for you. Once you decide on a Cardinal direction you want to stick with using that same orientation for the duration of your journey.

State this declaration before starting to set up your sacred space:

"I'm embarking on a journey that is sacred to all that I am. This journey reaches back to my very beginnings and to the essence of what and who I am. I remain open and willing to connect to my ancestors that came before me. My actions will be symbolic and true. I purposefully connect to those that are in my lineage. There is a path that brought me to this moment in time. It is unique and this journey will bring restoration and vigor to my life. It is my Sacred Journey."

PHASE 1-5

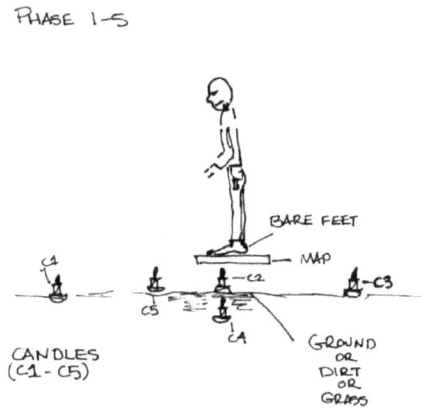

BARE FEET

MAP

CANDLES (C1 - C5)

GROUND OR DIRT OR GRASS

Area 1: Journey with the Earth

In this area you are connecting with the Earth itself. State the declaration, setup your space using the steps provided, and then follow the instructions.

1. State your declaration.

"I connect to the Earth the very vessel that gave shape and form to all living things in this physical realm. You are the sustainer of life, the keeper, and nurturer to us all. I move through your vast body and reestablish a rapport of a subtle nature."

2. Create your Sacred Space using the information above.
3. Step into the middle of your space with the fifth candle (your feet should be bare).
4. Face the appropriate direction.
5. Place the fifth candle on the ground or floor directly in front of you.
6. Light each candle starting with the top one and going full circle. Light the personal one last.
7. Calm and focus your thoughts, take a few deep breaths.
8. Join with the Earth by sensing or imagining a center vertical line, extending from your crown down through your feet and into the Earth.
9. Feel the connection going into the Earth and allow it to spread downward and outward as far as possible.
10. Close your physical eyes and allow yourself to move through the Earth using your senses. Remember the Physical Earth has several layers
11. Take your time and forge a solid connection with the Earth. Experiment by moving within the vastness of it. Do not try to go through the Earth's surface at any other point that will be for the next phase.
12. When you feel the connection is forged, you can use your senses or imagination to withdraw from the Earth. Move in reverse back along the route that you joined with it. Therefore move upward from the Earth, through your feet, and up to your crown. You should feel grounded (very relaxed and calm at this point.
13. Place all of your items back into your bundle until the next time.

The Earth is extremely vast and within it there are all types of rock and mineral formations, underground caves, underwater caverns, and many veins of water. As you move to different parts of it allow it to reacquaint with you. You are moving through it using the spiritual form that is held within a physical form. The physical form is made up of the same minerals that are within the Earth and it can resonate with it. Your spiritual body is transmitting information between the Earth and your physical body much like a telephone. Getting a feel for the things inside the Earth will help you when you are exploring the surface of the African continent.

Area 2: Journey to the African Continent

In this area you will be making a connection with the continent of Africa. You will again state a declaration, setup your Sacred Space, and follow the instructions given.

1. State your declaration.

"I connect to the continent and the womb that gave birth to mankind--A vast frontier of endless potential. I return to a home that I have not known on a conscious level. I draw vitality and strength from within her borders for she is the Motherland to all."

2. Create your Sacred Journey space
3. Step into the middle of your space with the fifth candle (your feet should be bare).
4. Face the appropriate direction.
5. Place the map of African continent under your feet and on top of the Earth itself. If you are taking your Sacred Journey indoors see "Alternative Procedures: In the Absence of Earth or Grass," because you will need to sprinkle some dirt on top of the map now. This means you are working on top of the cloth used for bundling your tools so that you protect the floor and can reuse the dirt.
6. Place the fifth candle on the ground or floor directly in front of you.
7. Light each candle starting with the top one and going full circle. Light the personal one last.
8. Calm and focus your thoughts, take a few deep breaths.
9. Quickly join with the Earth as you did in Phase 1.
10. Once you feel the connection with the Earth, move through it completely and come out or surface on the continent of Africa.

11. Move around the continent using your senses as in your first session when you moved through the Earth.
12. When you feel the connection with the continent is forged, you can return back up through the Earth, your feet, and to your crown area. You will feel as if you have gone somewhere exciting and new. There may also be a sense of amazement or wonderment.
13. Place all of your items back into your bundle until the next time.

The continent is vast, so you may want explore it more by repeating this connection several times. If your candles have been exhausted then you want to acquire more and prepare them as before.

Area 3: Journey with Your Ancestral Tribe

For this area you do not need consciously to go through the Earth because you surfaced above ground on the African continent in Phase 2. You will, therefore, take the position already being connected to the Earth and being located at a point near your ancestral village or in the center of the continent. This is what you have in mind when setting up your objects for making this journey. State the declaration again, setup your Sacred Space, and follow the instructions given.

1. State your declaration

"I will now connect and reunite with my ancestral village and tribesmen. They eagerly awaited my return. I will be able to find them quickly and easily. It will be a wonderful experience to explore and commune with my ancestors. This process and information will bring me into a state of wholeness and allow me to use my heritage to progress and prosper."

2. Create your Sacred Journey space.
3. Place the picture of Africa in the center of your designated area.

4. Sprinkle some dirt on top of it.
5. Step into the middle of your space with the fifth candle (your feet should be bare).
6. Face the appropriate direction.
7. Place the fifth candle on the ground directly in front of you.
8. Light each candle starting with the top one and going full circle. Light the personal one last.
9. Calm and focus your thoughts by taking a few deep breaths.
10. Join with the continent.
11. Allow your senses to move you to the location that your tribe once occupied.
12. Use your entire body to connect to and explore this area.
13. Once you have briefly explored the communal area, announce your presence to your tribesmen. This will allow their essence to come forth.
14. Make the following Declaration to your tribesmen.

"I am home, I have survived the Great Rift that once separated us, and I have returned home to the place and people of my ancestors."

15. This session must not be rushed. Allow your presence to be felt and embraced by your fellow tribesmen. The words you uttered and your presence must travel throughout the communal area. Young and old must be allowed to come near and commune with you. Your family will be told of your return, but you will not meet with them until the next phase.
16. When you feel the connection with your tribe has been forged; you may slowly disengage your connection with them. Let them know that you will return for more visits and to meet with your family. Tell them they are welcome to come and visit with you if they have a desire to do so. Upon completion of this phase you are left with the feeling that you have a crowd of people cheering for you and wishing you well. You feel that you had a visit with people that really wanted to be around you and see you succeed.
17. Gather all of your items back onto your cloth and bundle them until the next time.

18. If your candles have been exhausted then you want to acquire more and prepare them as before.

So much can be learned through the connection with this area. It would be very beneficial for you to revisit this area many times over. You can allow your tribesmen to escort you around the village when you return for more information. This meeting will be like showing up at an event, to an old neighborhood, or a holiday with family. People hear the commotion and come near. Once there everyone is saying who you are and who your family is. Many will relay old stories involving your family and important village events.

This is really your extended family unit. This is the group that is deeply connected to you and your family through ties other than blood. They will show you how they greet each other by greeting you so whatever they do you should readily do also. Some embrace with a hug, with a touch, or with a kiss, exchange of breath, with body movements, etc. It will be a joyous occasion

Please note that in this area you invited your ancestral tribesmen to visit with you. They will show up in different ways throughout your day or night however, if it alarms you, causes you anxiety or fear they will stop coming to interact with you. They tend to show their presence in the way that Angels do through aromas, animal/insect totems, or even people. They may also appear as figures or apparitions.

Make note of tribal information but do not incorporate it at this time. It is best to incorporate it after you have incorporated your family's information.

Area 4: Journey with Your Ancestral Family

In this area you will be making the connection with your ancestral families. Your connections with the Earth, the continent, and tribesmen remain intact. You can set up and start this phase of your Sacred Journey in the communal village of your ancestral tribe.

It is best to pick a location near your ancestral village or at the center of it. You will again state a declaration, setup your Sacred Space, and follow the instructions given.

1.   State your declaration.

"I will now connect and reunite with my ancestral family. They have eagerly awaited my return. I will be able to find them quickly and easily. It will be a wonderful experience that will allow me to gain much information. This process and information will bring me into a state of wholeness and allow me to use my heritage to progress and prosper."

2.   Create your Sacred Journey space.
3.   Place the picture of Africa in the center of your designated area.
4.   Sprinkle some dirt on top of it.
5.   Step into the middle of your space with the fifth candle (your feet should be bare).
6.   Face the appropriate direction.
7.   Place the fifth candle on the ground directly in front of you.
8.   Light each candle starting with the top one and going full circle. Light the personal one last.
9.   Calm and focus your thoughts by taking a few deep breaths.
10. Standing in the middle of your tribal village, reconnect with your tribe using your entire being. They have been waiting for you and wish to lead you to your family.
11. Follow along with them joyfully to your family's home. It will be the home of the eldest member of your ancestral family.
12. Once outside the home, announce yourself as you did to the village.

Make the following Declaration.

"My beloved family, I am home once again. I have survived the Great and terrible Rift that separated us so long ago, but now I have returned home to the people and place of my ancestors."

13. Meet with the eldest family member. She or he will release you to meet with the rest of the family.
14. Once released by the eldest family member, allow others to meet and commune with you. Allow them to embrace you and celebrate your return.
15. When you are ready to return from this connection let them know you will come back and that they are free to come visit with you.
16. Place all of your items back onto your cloth and bundle it until the next time.

You are able to gain so much knowledge concerning your ancestral past through this area of your journey. Much information will be shown to you each time you move along this path. It is important to make note of all that you can remember. It is okay if you do not remember everything. The excitement and awe of it will sweep you away but being able to return here and to have your ancestors come to you will more than compensate for anything that is lost in the moment.

If you received the information concerning your family's colors, crest, animal, etc., you can incorporate it now. You can use the family's colors for your candles if you choose to but continue to use a white candle (C5 personal candle), to represent yourself. If your candles have been exhausted or you choose to use colored candles then you want to acquire them and prepare them as before.

Area 5: Journey with Divine Source

In this area of the journey you will be re-forging the connection you have with Divine Source. You want to take a relaxed position that allows you to watch the glass or bowl which may mean using a chair and table/stand (see Alternative Procedures Phase V). We use liquids to simulate the movement and the interaction of you with Divine Source. The food color represents you and the water represents Divine Source. The color is acting as your physical form, which allows you to track your movements and interactions with the Divine.   The clear water acts as Divine Source, which remains unseen, constant, and all around you.

The two liquids will move and interact until they become totally merged…until they not only move as one, but also are one. The goal in this area is for you to experience the state of true Oneness with Divine Source. You must be reacquainted with the feel of it until it is second nature. This is the best position to take when seeking information concerning your ancestral path.

PHASE 5

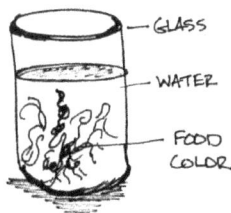

1.   State the opening declaration

"I reconnect with the Infinite Divine Source of all. I open all levels of my mind and my being to the Divine Source of all things and all matter."

2.   Create the Sacred Journey space
3.   Place a small table/stand in the center along with a chair (see Alternative Procedure-Phase V Sitting Position for details)
4.   Fill the glass or bowl with water within 1-2 inches from the top. The water represents Divine Source.
5.   Hold the container in front of you if you like but it is better to use a small table/stand so that you avoid getting fatigued.
6.   Drop 1 good-sized squirt or ¼ - ½ tsp of food color into the water. The food color represents you.
7.   Do not mix but allow the food color disperse on its own.

8. Take your position within the Sacred Journey space & place the container on the table/stand.
9. Constantly watch the contents of the container and mimic the motions of the food color using your mind and being. This represents your interaction with Divine Source.
10. Allow yourself to relax into the movement of the food color.
11. You should feel the outward moving of your being in a fluid manner.
12. As you sense and feel the movement, focus your attention on the perimeter of your being (This is the area furthest from you).
13. Intend and allow a conscious connection between you and Divine Source to form and weave together.
14. Consciously intend and allow this connection to continue inward from all directions until it reaches its centermost point of your being.
15. Send your conscious thought and intent outward in all directions to the perimeter.
16. Repeat steps 8-11 several times until you cannot sense a distinguished perimeter.
17. When you no longer sense a distinguished perimeter, come back to the center (you), and sit quietly for a bit in this renewed state of oneness.
18. Your connection with Divine Source has been re-established.
19. State the ending declaration:

"All levels, all realms, and all dimensions are now open to me. I have full access to the infinite knowledge. The Infinite Divine Source is in all and part of all. My entire being is one with Infinite Divine Source. I am one with all there is. I am one with this moment in time and from here the Universe opens up to me. I move through time in any direction or dimension along my ancestral path with the greatest ease."

20. Place all of your items back onto your cloth and bundle it until the next time.

The vital connection to each area of your Sacred Journey has been made. You can return to any and all areas to explore and glean information as many times as you like. This will help you in your move forward. You are trying to learn about yourself through others. You are the result of the people, customs, environment, and things that you came before you. Observe them with a childlike curiosity because they may seem quite strange and different from anything that you know.

Chapter 19

Alternative Procedures

I have taken into account a few varying situations for those desiring to embark on their Sacred Journey. Please understand that all of the information provided in this book are not hard and fast rules. They have been provided as introductory information and can be altered if and when needed. The information in this chapter is for instance when an individual needs to sit instead of stand. There is also information for those that do not have immediate access to the ground.

Sitting Position

This method can be used for all regular Phases and areas if the individual has difficulty standing. You will be placing a chair or stool in the center of the space you will be using then following the normal procedures of the phase.

1. Place a chair or stool in the center of the space you will be using. Situate the chair so that it is facing the appropriate direction (the standing direction you will be using).
2. Items that would be placed in the center of the space are placed directly in front of the chair and the other items will be set in place around the chair
3. Continue from step three of the appropriate Phase

Sitting Position (Phase V)

Set up your sacred space according to the Phase V and follow the instructions there. This is to further explain step three. The map and personal candle are optional in this Phase. It can be place in front of the map (under the table), in front of the table, next to the table, or on top of the table (see diagram). Keep in mind that the flickering flame of the personal candle may distract you if it is placed on top of the table.

1. Place a chair or stool in the center of the space you will be using. Situate the chair so that it is facing the appropriate direction (the standing direction you will be using).
2. Place a small table or stand in front of the chair. You are going to place the glass on top of this table or stool so that you are able to observe it without getting fatigued.
3. The personal candle C5 are can be place in a spot that you are comfortable with. On the table/stand, under the table, or in front of the table. Just make sure it is in a safe spot and will not be knocked over.
4. Continue from step four of Phase V.

Phase V Sitting Position

In the Absence of Earth or Grass

This method is used indoors or outdoors for Phases 1-5 if no earth or grass is present.

In preparation for this you will need to place your bundle on the earth in advance. This can be done while sitting on a park bench, at the beach/lake, or any place that allows you access to the earth. When connecting to the Earth through the dirt you will need to picture or imagine some place real where the natural Earth is. Do not see the real wood, carpet, concrete, asphalt, or indoor position you are occupying because you are relocating yourself to the continent of Africa

Please carefully note the diagram. You will lay the bundle cloth on top of the floor. Lay the dirt on top of the bundle cloth. Lay the map on top of the dirt. You will then step on top of the map. This will simulate you standing on the ground in Africa.

Standing Position

1. Put the Locator in your pocket or on your person
2. Determine the cardinal direction you are going to use and locate it using the compass.
3. Place your four candles in position. This means each should be in a cardinal direction. The fifth candle represents you and is put in position once you are in place within the Sacred Space of the candles.
4. Place the cloth from your bundle on floor or ground in the middle of your area to protect the surface and keep the soil for future use.
5. Pour the dirt on top of it and spread it out enough so that it will be under both feet at once. If doing Phase 2 or 3 save a little of the dirt to use later.
6. Step inside the designated area facing the appropriate directions

7. Continue from Step Three of the appropriate Phase
8. When finished pour dirt back into a Ziploc bag for use later.
9. Shake excess dirt off cloth.
10. Place all items back onto the cloth, bundle, and store

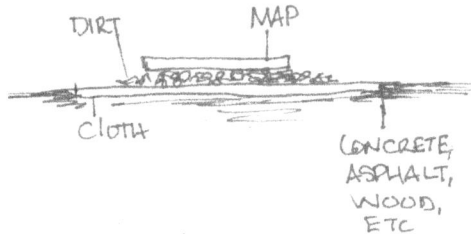

Sitting Position

1. Put the Locator in your pocket or on your person
2. Determine the cardinal direction you are going to use and locate it using the compass.
3. Place a chair or stool inside the designated area facing the appropriate direction.
4. Place your four candles in position. This means each candle should be in a cardinal direction. The fifth candle represents you and is put in position once you are in place within the Sacred Space of the candles.
5. Place cloth from your bundle on floor or ground in front of the chair or stool to protect the surface and keep the soil for future use.
6. Pour the dirt on top of it and spread it out enough so that it will be under both feet at once. If doing Phase 2 or 3 save a little of the dirt to use later.
7. Step inside and sit in the chair or on the stool
8. Continue from step three of the appropriate Phase
9. When finished pour dirt back into a Ziploc bag for use later.
10. Shake excess dirt off cloth.
11. Place all items back onto the cloth, bundle, and store

Partnering Up

This method can be used to accommodate many individuals at one time but for the initial journey there should be no more than four.

All individuals using this method MUST be from the same MATERNAL bloodline. This is the strongest bloodline and it produces the truest results. Most people see feminine as the nurturing caregiver but the Universal Feminine is the creative life giver. It is the womb where the explosion of all life starts and we want to move along that line with purpose and intent. We can make stops anywhere along that line and take little detours to fill in information concerning anything of interest.

Some people may feel more comfortable taking their journey with someone else. You can approach a family member by asking them to help you explore a process that may prove beneficial to the healing process of your family. Much of the information presented is new and very different from anything they may have experienced before. Many may find this new terrain a bit unsettling and may want to start out by working with another person.

The ideal partner is one from your maternal bloodline and cannot be a friend, associate, or from your paternal bloodline. The maximum number of people occupying a space constructed for a Sacred Journey is four. There are a few differences when partnering up and space is a key factor for using this procedure. The construction of the space must be large enough for everyone to fit in it comfortably.

This method requires everyone to work together throughout the course of Sacred Journey without feeling rushed. Each phase and area is entered and left together. All individuals can occupy the same prepared space but face a different direction if they choose to. The activities of each phase and area are carried out by each individual for example: each would light a personal candle, state the declaration, work with a Locator, receive information, etc.

This procedure allows an individual to take his or her Sacred Journey while being accompanied by others. It also provides an interesting opportunity to compare notes and exchange information that was received during each area. Each person will use his or her own bundle with one exception. The four candles used to set the Sacred Space are shared by all partners.

Each person:
- Must fit within the constructed space at the same time
- Must have and use his or her own bundle of tools (except the four candles used to construct the sacred space)
- Should face the direction of his or her choice
- Declarations are spoken together
- Phases and areas are entered and exited together (no one must feel rushed to finish a session)

Partners facing the same direction

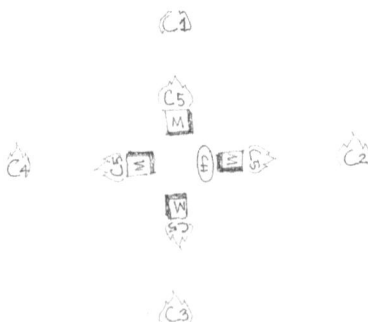

Partners facing different directions

PART IV

CONTINUING THE JOURNEY

Chapter 20

Journeying Back

Each return trip along your Sacred Journey will bring new and wonderful information about your lineage. Sometimes it seems like a storybook unfolding right before your eyes and at other times it seems like you are taking part of a magical book full of adventures. Sacred Journey Africa gives you a passport that provides you with unlimited access. You can take as many return trips back to each area if you choose to. You can go as often as you like.

Reconnect Process

There is not need to use the setup for a reconnect session unless you choose to or feel it is necessary. If you find it difficult to get information, connect, or get in touch with tribesmen or ancestors then you can set up the sacred space. Sometimes your connection is good but you and your ancestors are use to the sacred space. This is because in creating a sacred space it helps to block out interferences.

Method 1:

1.   Dig a slight hole or clear a space on the ground large enough for both feet to fit at one time (bare feet). If no natural earth is available use an Alternate Method.
2.   Stand in the space.

3.   Join with Earth, continent, tribe, or ancestors
4.   State Declaration (connection): *"I and (the Earth, continent, tribe, or my ancestors) are connected. I call up that connection now. Guide me and show me the answer to the information I seek."*
5.   Sense the connection
6. Repeat connection declaration for each connection

Method 2:

If you feel your connections with the areas are strong then you can omit having to stand on dirt.

1. Stand in the space.
2. Join with Earth, continent, tribe, or ancestors
3. State Declaration (connection): *"I and (the Earth, continent, tribe, or my ancestors) are connected. I call up that connection now. Guide me and show me the answer to the information I seek."*
4. Sense the connection
5. Repeat connection declaration for each connection

Chapter 21

Asking Questions

People or groups oftentimes migrated around the continent. Your questions should be simple and as direct as possible. You must communicate through pictures and a sense of knowing or sensing, so that you can hear. You will be using your intuitive, spiritual senses and discernment. Maintain focus or you may get frustrated and shut the door of communication. Understand that where you were born can be quite different from where your ancestors were born. Additionally different generations may have settled in different locations.

When you are contacting ancestors, there can be two different sets of answers for each person you contact. If you word your questions for a group or tribe the answers you get may be more general in nature. These will provide a good starting point for you. Keep in mind that although they are general in nature some neighboring tribes also comingled. Many of the tribes that traveled around the continent as well as the tribes that went about pillaging and fighting would also comingle.

It is always good to start your quest for answers with asking general questions then move on to more specific ones. When asking specific questions be clear as to the maternal or paternal side. For example, I will ask a question concerning the family's trade. This would be the type of work the family did to make a living. If this is asked concerning the generation before me, the question would be general and contain information about my mother and father.

Question: What was the family trade?
Answer: Dietician, cleaning, construction

The answers I received reflect the line of work and two business ventures. This is because I did not specify maternal or paternal therefore I received three answers. I would need to be more specific with the questions that I ask if I want information concerning just my mother's line or just my father's line.

Once I receive an answer I could ask more questions along that part of the family line. If I was to focus on another generation back along the family line, I would still need to pose my questions as to the maternal or paternal side of the family. I would then do as before and follow along one line at a time.

You should keep a journal and maybe use a diagram to place ancestors on as you gain that information. The information you receive helps to give you insight into your distant past. You may not receive names but you may receive sounds or pictures relating to a name.

The main goal is to receive background information that will show you what you are made of. Remember that at first you may want to communicate by using pictures. Ask questions focusing on one thing at a time and wait for answers. Avoid making up answers or losing patience. This process is to help you bridge the gap between you and your ancestors. You want to go away from this experience in a position of wholeness.

You can regain a connection that has been lost for centuries. Your heritage keeps you from feeling and living like an island. We cannot all retrace our roots like the author Alex Haley did some years back. There are skeletons in many closets that may never be revealed during the light of day. Using the techniques presented here can help provide you with enough information that those skeletons will not matter.

These techniques are for reconnecting with ancestors from past centuries. These techniques work particularly well for connecting with those that came before the "Great Rift." The "Great Rift" would be time coupled with the events that tore ancestor from ancestor. It caused many to be displaced through slavery and bondage. It caused a heritage to be striped away and discarded as though it had no meaning. It was in fact, the beginning of a genocidal movement that continues even today.

Chapter 22

Locating Things

To locate places, people or things of your past you will need the map and Locator. Keep your writing instrument and journal close by so you can mark your map or take notes. I guarantee you will not remember all of the information that you receive. You may receive bits and pieces of information like pieces of a puzzle. It is usually best to not get overly excited so that you will not stop the flow of information and so that you can jot down quick notes or make picture markings on your map.

You may also want to create your own shorthand symbols or legend on the map. For instance, stick people or a head to represent a person. You could make two for a couple or three for a group or tribe. You can also use arrowheads for houses, wavy lines for water, spears, or arrows for hunting and so on. Pictures are the universal language.

If you develop a shorthand system it helps you speak in pictures. Do not belabor it though, because the symbols will come to you in time and they may also change. Focus your attention first on certain pictures and their meanings as you communicate with your ancestors you will learn their language.

Locating Objects

This is your starting position for asking any question. Always assume this position before asking a question.

Physical Starting Position:
1. Place the map in front of you on the cloth.
2. Sit on the floor or in a chair at a table.
3. Assume a comfortable position.
4. Hold the Locator by its handle allowing the body and head to hang free.
5. Make sure you have plenty of room for it to move freely.
6. Center the head over the continent.
7. If you use a suggestion card then position the Locator in a neutral starting point (see diagram).

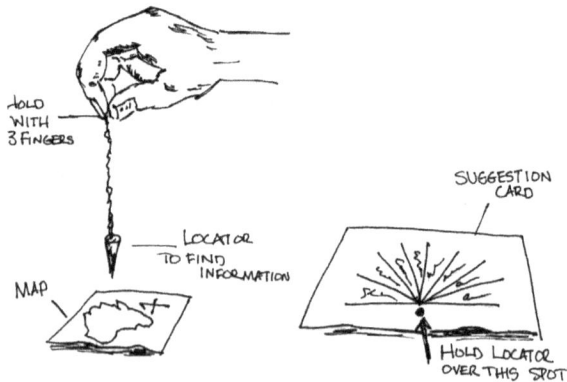

If the Locator swings clockwise or counter clockwise over the entire map or suggestion card when you assume the starting position it is okay. Just allow it to come to a complete stop on its own before you proceed.

Mental Position

Anytime you want to work with the Locator you must start with a clear, calm, and quiet mind. Your mood should be pleasant, happy, or even-toned. The receptive position is to be cooperative and to carry on in an "Ask & Receive" train of thought. Avoid questioning in disbelief, becoming offended, or taking a defensive position to the information that the Locator displays. Those positions will cause information to stop flowing to you.

Some information you receive may potentially shock you but just make a note of it and keep moving. The Locator may swing, lean, or pull in a direction along the map. When it does that you want to slowly move it in the direction of the swinging or pulling motion. Take your time moving slowly so you do not overshoot the location that it is trying to show you. If you do pass the location the Locator will gently pull in the opposite direction. If it is guiding you some place you may need to take a series of turns.

Use your sense of sight and touch together when working with the Locator. The more you work with it the more sensitive you become to how it moves. If it stops leaning or pull and stands straight, you have located the spot. It may also swing over a spot that you are trying to locate as well. If the Locator moves around frantically as if it is trembling or wandering, then you must calm your inner thoughts.

Try to focus on one question at a time and do not race back and forth between questions. Avoid moving too quickly to the next question or becoming fearful. Also remember not to move back and forth from asking the Locator a question then supplying your own negative or doubt-filled answer. Your thoughts can move at a speed that is faster than lightening. Each thought creates an energetic movement (a vibration), that can be sensed and picked up by the Locator.

The Locator will display a fidgety nervous movement when your thoughts move around unfocused or on multiple things. Always be aware of the invisible vertical plum line that exists when you hold the Locator in an extended fashion by the handle. Any movement or slant of the Locator past the invisible plum line is a guiding that you should follow in the direction of the pull.

If the Locator displays a pulling, tugging, or leaning motion, follow in the direction of the leading.

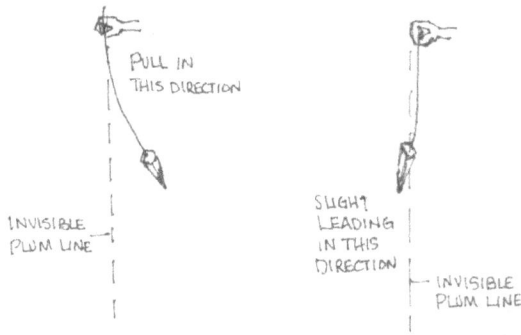

PULL IN
THIS DIRECTION

INVISIBLE
PLUM LINE

SLIGHT
LEADING
IN THIS
DIRECTION

INVISIBLE
PLUM LINE

If the Locator displays a strange or uneven swinging motion you must follow it in the direction of the greatest or longest swing

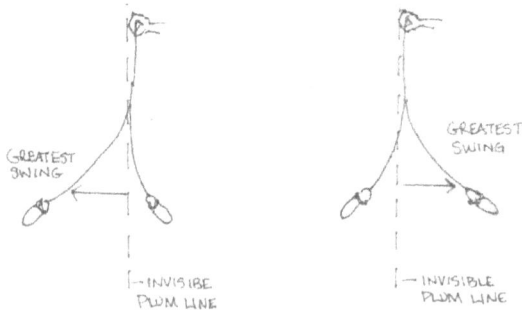

GREATEST
SWING

GREATEST
SWING

INVISIBLE
PLUM LINE

INVISIBLE
PLUM LINE

If it moves frantically or shake nervously along the plum line you must calm your thoughts, focus on one question, and rid yourself of fear.

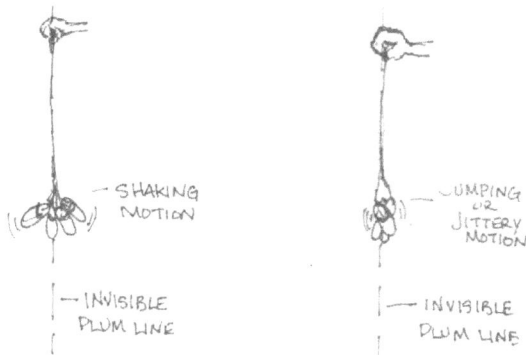

When asking Yes or No type questions refer to the programming Locator information. Focus and ask one question at a time. You can ask a series of questions along a specific line but only ask one question at a time. Sometimes you may need to rephrase your question to get the answer you seek. For instance, where did my ancestors live? You could have had seven or more generations preceding the "Great Rift." That would mean many people in that space of time.

If you asked about grand parents then that would mean four grand parents per generation. You must find a way to word your questions so you get the answers you seek and move through the generations of your ancestors. You can start at the "Great Rift" and move backwards. Be sure to make notes concerning them to help you keep the information straight.

Chapter 23

Identify the Land

Since the continent has changed so much in the last few centuries, it would be difficult to locate the precise area that you are from. Making a connection with the land would be easy if you were able to trace your family tree back to its earliest known origins. You may however receive information that you may be able to research through historical data, art, or museums. The historical data may be somewhat sketchy and sparse.

Art history books and museums contain information that has been classified as art but was not intended or used for that purpose. Usually these venues will have some relevant information that can point out locations, customs, and people. Do not dismiss the information (images) as trivial because they could be vital landmarks for specific areas. Anything could act as a landmark for instance a tree/stump, stone; bend in the road, water source, sign/post, or marking.

You can still reconnect to the land by analyzing your known ancestors, your likes, dislikes and sensing. For instance, most people, having relocated, will still do what they know to do. If they are skilled in a particular area, they try to gain employment in that area. Brick mason do not try to lay carpets or farm crops. If a person cannot find work in their field, then he or she will try a different field to survive. Chefs look for cooking jobs, seamstresses, or tailors look for jobs dealing with making or repairing clothes and so on.

My maternal ancestors were fisherman through and through as far back as we can trace. They came from colder climates and knew the water like the backs of their hands. The women were skilled in holistic medicine and midwifery. My paternal ancestors knew about raising crops and animals. They were also good mechanical engineers.

Analyzing the information gathered concerning them shows that my maternal ancestors had to have had access to a body of water or the ocean along with a variety of plants that could be used as medicine. The area would have bordered the ocean because the sea seemed to call to them but with a great deal of vegetation. These ancestors could tell us about storms, marine life, problem solving, farming/gardening, aromatherapy, and holistic medicines.

My paternal ancestors possessed skills and knowledge needed to grow crops and it is possible that they came from a region that provided an area conducive to growing crops. Since the ones from two generations past seemed to be able to grow any type of crops anywhere, the land may not have seemed ideal to others for raising crops.

Check out what types of environments call to you or which environments you prefer to be in. I have a love for growing things and the ocean draws me with calls from a deep place within. I cannot locate the source of the calls, but they come with pictures, scents, and sounds. I cannot be land-locked for long periods of time without feeling imprisoned. When I go on vacation, I almost always dip my feet in the ocean, river, or both.

Some people have to be around plants or flowers and some people cannot grow a plant to save their own life. Some people are drawn to animals and others must work with their hands (glass, wood, metal, clay, etc.). There are people that have a constant flow of music or chatter bursting from within. These are the natural born musicians and communicators.

Artisans are those that must create using their hands; people with a love of the land, trees, or plants may be the builders, farmers, guides, holistic caregivers and nomads. The fisherman not only loves and needs to be around water, but also is drawn by it. The herdsmen are those that have a love and passion for animals.

Chapter 24

Identify the People

The African continent was filled with many materials in their natural or raw form. Everything had to be manufactured without the use of machinery. A community needed craftsmen of every imaginable caliber if it was to survive. There were very few specialists because each person had to fulfill many different duties. Each community had its hierarchy system which may or may not have been elaborate.

The common goal was the success and survival of the community. This may have been the driving force behind cooperation and camaraderie of the people. Certain studies and investigations have shown that the present landscape is far from what it was hundreds of years ago. Therefore, trying to match oneself to a specific, modern location may not render the desired results. If you cannot locate an old rendering, it will be best to stick to a region.

From elders, judges, hunters, gatherers, farmers, herdsmen to artisans, each community had its own set of rules or laws, as well as standards that established financial classes.   Although they were skilled in many areas as a way of making sure the community had all that it needed, they may still have lacked certain items because of their location.

There were many that were also what we now call entrepreneurs. They often traveled near and far to trade what was abundant in their community with other communities. Take note of the types of items (headdress, garments, jewelry, weapons), and what they were made of (shell, wood, metal, ceramic, grass, reed, cloth, animal).   Other things that are equally important are piercings, scaring of skin/body, manipulation/elongating of body parts.

Chapter 25

Identify the Customs

Many of the actions, habits, and customs displayed by present-day African-Americans are the products of their environment and many years of manipulative programming. Many appear to be lazy and of low moral character and fortitude. They appear to be self-centered, neglectful of their young, abusive and unfaithful to their mates. They display a propensity for violence and lack the ability to be taught or to excel in areas of higher learning.

They have been stripped of their own heritage and forced to become chameleons. If not for the aforementioned things, you would see that they are a race that is far from being lazy, immoral, or savage. This is a proud race that is driven by deep seeded emotions and instincts. Their core houses the survival mechanism for themselves and their young.

Despite mass media's portrayal of them this race of people truly cares for and nurtures their young. They are quick to assist and mentor those in need. They are of the mind that it takes an entire village to raise their young. This means that a person becomes the best adult possible when all those in the village contribute to the upbringing of each person.

You see they were of the mind that every adult within the village has something he or she can impart and teach the young, so that the entire community benefits when the young become adults. They respect the elders of the community and feel their wisdom is needed continually to help guide the community and teach on its history. Their young bring hope and an energy that is vibrant and promising. Each child eagerly goes from adult to adult, absorbing all that he or she is exposed to, like a sponge. Mature adults carry out the traditions of the community and replenish it; each individual doing his or her part to build the community and keep it running smoothly and productively.

This is a race that has very strong moral character, compassionate and uses brute force, only if it feels it is necessary. They are the foundational building blocks for all humanity. Their bodily structure and color contain all that is needed to produce a very wide variety of results. They are friendly and within their make-up is the ability to easily connect with Source.

They also have an uncanny ability to easily adapt and master things and situations, which is what strikes fear in many others. This fear is why others felt the need to strip them of everything, including their God. They have been given half-truths, bits, and pieces of information and a target goal to strive for. Their willingness to trust and see the good in others is one thing that keeps them from seeing that the information that is presented to them is not entirely true and that it continues to change.

The true information remains hidden and they are constantly being suppressed and oppressed even in this day and age. The old traditional customs that a community may have had were usually ritualistic in nature to the point of being religious. These could range from ordinary to extreme. They could involve marking, piercing, and painting the body, dyeing the hair and mouth, elongating the neck, ears, lips, head, or waist.

Group dancing for funerals, weddings, or other ceremonies, feasting on the blood of an animal or allowing others to beat you with reeds, leather, sticks, stones, etc. or walking on hot coals or broken glass was also part of some tribal customs. Today, in these modern times, the customs are still ritualistic in nature to the point of being religious. Dancing is done for pleasure and showmanship.

At times, it is used in place of fighting. In some places, it is thought to be odd or shameful if one does not know how to do the latest dance styles. If a person does not have rhythm, they are criticized. Circumcision was once just a religious custom. It is now customary to circumcise male children at birth due to health reasons.

Society has passed specific laws or stated certain customs, such as marrying before having children. Some present dowries or rings in contemplation of marriage. The father presents the bride to the groom during the wedding ceremony. Gifts are given for almost every occasion, and the list goes on.

Keep note of the slightest information because it can be quite valuable. Customs can be something as simple as tribes or people getting together to exchange gifts. Many people have customs that involve carrying figurines that look like statues or dolls. They are used as an aide to assist them with everything from contacting god (like modern day saints), prosperous harvests, village well-being, trying to conceive a child, to coping with life's struggles and situations.

Chapter 26

Identifying Mascots and Symbols

Many communities selected something to act as a representation of them as a whole. It could have been anything (color, flower, etc.) or any animal they regarded as meaningful, powerful, or sacred. They would paint their bodies, especially during ceremonies, to resemble these symbols. Oftentimes, they would use parts of the animal for clothing, weapons, adornments (jewelry, hair, headdresses, etc.). Statues, markings and other items resembling the community's sacred symbol are placed in various locations throughout the community to bestow blessings of health and success.

We see this today, where a nation, state, providence, city, organization or family uses a symbol to set them apart from others. These symbols also make it quite easy to identify those that it is associated with. These picture symbols are generally called trademarks or logos now, and are so widely used that they may appear without any words. These symbols are not the same as totems, but they can help to instill confidence.

In cases when the symbol is representative of a religious entity, it may also help by providing a point of contact, guidance, comfort, protection, hope, faith, etc. In some communities, only the priests, shaman, witchdoctor, medicine man, or medicine woman worked closely with the spirit realm and the natural world. They are not so prevalent today or accessible; if they were, they did not do what we are attempting to do here.

Within a Sacred Journey we do a merging of sorts when working with symbols. The symbol will help reconnect you with the valuable essence of your past and instill confidence in you. It can also help guide your actions and thought process so that you make better decisions for your life. The symbol will act as a point of contact to reconnect old (ancestors) with the new (you). Your true potential may remain dormant and untapped because you have been disconnected from the essence of who you really are.

When you observe animals, you will notice that much is taught through demonstration. The young will often display an unflinching boldness and confidence when their parent or family group is near. When a baby is venturing out to test his or her limits, he or she also displays these traits when an older sibling or adult is near.

When loved ones leave home or a family is separated for various reasons, there continues to be an invisible bond. If communication between family and friends is lost for years, there still remains that invisible bond. Though the physical cord of connection no longer exists an etheric one is ever present. Most are unaware of it and therefore never seek it out.

It is said that over time, even the invisible connection dissipates. I do not believe it dissipates completely, though; especially when one feels their days on this planet are coming to an end. They often send out prayers and well wishes for many of their loved ones. If everything is energy and energy is never lost, but merely changing forms, then the connection is not lost either. It may have been stretched quite thin over a great distance, but, never the less, it still exists.

Chapter 27

Identify the Ancestors

Identifying your ancestors is the same as trying to pinpoint an area on the continent. You want to examine the ancestors you have access to. Examine all of the information that was passed to you through stories or the memories of other family members. Be sure to examine for yourself. This information helps to give you a point to connect with.

Remember some families tend to pass on the knowledge and skills that they have acquired. It is a great low cost way to give the next generation a jump-start to providing for their families. There are many, many opportunities open to each individual. In this country a person is free to decide his or her own career path. I must say, participating in a family business can only help you and your family as you gain knowledge and skills in other areas, even if it is not your career choice, it can still help you in another area.

Knowing things about your ancestors is like completing a piece of a puzzle. These missing pieces will help you discover who you are or what you came from. This is vitally important to you and the race you are a member of if you desire to truly succeed and make a difference in the life that you live or in the lives of those connected to you in some way.

PART V

BENEFITS OF THE JOURNEY

Chapter 28

Future Journeys

You do not have to redo the initial connection steps carried out in each Phase unless you choose to. You can go directly to any point in your ancestral past that you like. I recommend returning to each leg of the Sacred Journey to explore it further. Doing so helps to continually build the invisible foundation that was lost for so long.

There is much to see and learn about your past and your ancestors will be happy to share the information. It would also be good to recite the Final Declaration aloud from time to time. Enjoy traveling along your Sacred Journey, it is a journey back through your ancestral past that will help you move through this lifetime and forge the way for future generations.

In reality, you have always been linked to your ancestors through the invisible threads of DNA both physical and spiritual as well as through time. You may have been unaware of them or unable to fully make use of them but you have always been connected to your ancestors and the Infinite Divine Source of all things. It is a connection that can be neglected, forgotten, ignored, overlooked, or re-established, but it cannot be broken. The connection is very important when seeking information that has been lost, hidden, or out of reach.

So many people are unaware of this connection because of the numerous distractions that are present in their lives. In a vast number of societies the elderly are not considered a top priority and are tossed aside as if they were a pair of old shoes. The societies that do recognize their value keep the elderly close and are able to give a wise guiding light to their young. In those that hold Divine Source as part of their religious practices, usually teach that you must reach out into the great beyond with prayers and petitions. The true connection is part of an invisible but infinite thread. This infinite part (soul or spirit), has no shape or form and no beginning or end.

If you look closely as some have done, you will find that something, which fits that description, is within you. No one knows how to keep it or trap it. Many ways have been found to force it out of a physical body, but the exact time it leaves can only be approximated. Once it leaves the body, everything concerning it becomes an even greater mystery.

This new reconnected position is unique and there is no other position like it. Things are seen and interpreted differently from this perspective. In this new position, you take on the mind and sight of the Infinite One with the full guidance of your ancestors. You are able to see things in a new way and your perception of them also changes. You lived life from the lowly position of a human and this position is the highest one you can take. This was your true beginning and it is the end of your Sacred Journey.

Final Declaration

Though many fear and come against us from all sides,

Nothing and no one is lost,

All is restored.

Blessed are my ancestors,

Blessed are my kinsmen throughout my family line,

And blessed are my tribesmen.

From generation to generation we reconnect and move as one.

We stretch and move through infinite time and space

We reconnect and work together.

We take heed to learn from past victories and past mistakes

As we reunite, move in unison and work as one,

We are made whole and our strength is restored.

We take charge of our lives and the situations within them

We are truly a blessed and prosperous race.

Chapter 29

The Journey Forward

It is a travesty and an injustice if a race loses the traditions that are normally interwoven through the daily lives of its people. The sad fact is that traditions can be totally lost to a race if only one generation is without them. These traditions are like the threads of a garment. They not only are the stitches that bind the garment together but they are interlaced to create the very fabric that makes up the garment.

All traditions are not necessary but some are and others tend to morph and change as the years pass. Most of us live in a country where the only traditions we have are getting together on a holiday to eat or exchange gifts.

Sacred Journey Africa will help you reconnect spiritually to your ancestors and through that connection you, your family, and your generation can bring back some of the traditions that contain echoes from your past ancestors. Those traditions had a more valuable purpose. They helped instill pride, confidence, self-esteem, and knowledge. History moves in cycles and therefore it is always repeating itself. Each new cycle tends to yield results that are either better or worst than the previous one. It one does not educate himself or herself then when a cycle repeats he or she will feel the affects are worst than ever before.

Most people tend to believe what others say and never pick up a book or research a subject. When you search out information you are more likely to find the truth or something close to it. If you take the word of others you will most likely get information that is shaped by their opinions, biases, and beliefs.

It is my hope that you are made whole through the use of this information. It is my sincere wish that you have gained the valuable and priceless tools that can be forged into traditions that you are proud to pass on to the future generations. Your life's journey moving forward will be more fulfilling and enjoyable by incorporating what you have gleamed from your on Sacred Journey.

I bid you Universal Peace, Prosperity, and Blessings with Long Life, and Adventure Filled Journeys!

Appendix

List of Items

Cloth – *White, approximately 1 yard*
Locator *(purchased or made)*
Compass
Bottle of water - *unopened*
Clear glass or clear bowl
Food Color – *Blue or Green*
5 White Candles
5 Clear candleholders - *Foil can be used if performing phase outside*
Picture of Africa – *8 x 10 or larger*
Writing instrument - *pen, pencil, or marker*
Notepad/Journal
Dirt
Blank paper (unlined) - *few pieces*

Declarations

For use when dedicating your bundle:

"I dedicate these items that lie before me to the purpose of helping me complete my Sacred Journey that will connect me to my ancestors and restore to me my full and rightful heritage that will help me successfully move through this life."

Use when asking for assistance for your Sacred Journey

"I, your name ask the entities that you seek assistance from to assist me in quickly and successfully completing this Sacred Journey that will reconnect me with my ancestors and restore to me my true and rightful heritage that will help me successfully travel through this life. Thank you for your assistance with this matter."

Use when beginning your Sacred Journey

"I'm embarking on a journey that is sacred to all that I am. This journey reaches back to my very beginnings and to the essence of what and who I am. I remain open and willing to connect to my ancestors that came before me. My actions will be symbolic and true. I purposefully connect to those that are in my lineage. There is a path that brought me to this moment in time. It is unique and this journey will bring restoration and vigor to my life. It is my Sacred Journey."

Phase 1 The Earth

"I connect to the Earth the very vessel that gave shape and form to all living things in this physical realm. You are the sustainer of life, the keeper, and nurturer to us all. I move through your vast body and reestablish a rapport of a subtle nature."

Phase 2 African Continent

"I connect to the continent that gave birth to mankind--A vast frontier of endless potential. I return to a home that I have not known on a conscious level. I draw vitality and strength from within her borders for she is the Motherland to all."

Phase 3 Tribe

"I will now connect and reunite with my ancestral village and tribesmen. They eagerly awaited my return. I will be able to find them quickly and easily. It will be a wonderful experience to explore and commune with my ancestors. This process and information will bring me into a state of wholeness and allow me to use my heritage to progress and prosper."

When greeting your Ancestral Tribesmen

"I am home, I have survived the Great Rift that once separated us, and I have returned home to the place and people of my ancestors."

Phase 4 Ancestral Family

"I will now connect and reunite with my ancestral family. They have eagerly awaited my return. I will be able to find them quickly and easily. It will be a wonderful experience that will allow me to gain much information. This process and information will bring me into a state of wholeness and allow me to use my heritage to progress and prosper."

Use when greeting Ancestral Family

"My beloved family, I am home once again. I have survived the Great and terrible Rift that separated us so long ago, but now I have returned home to the people and place of my ancestors."

Phase V Divine Source

"I reconnect with the Infinite Divine Source of all. I open all levels of my mind and my being to the Divine Source of all things and all matter."

Use at the end of Phase V

"All levels, all realms, and all dimensions are now open to me. I have full access to the infinite knowledge. The Infinite Divine Source is in all and part of all. My entire being is one with Infinite Divine Source. I am one with all there is. I am one with this moment in time and from here the Universe opens up to me. I move through time in any direction or dimension along my ancestral path with the greatest ease."

Reconnecting

> *"I and (the Earth, continent, tribe, or my ancestors) are connected. I call up that connection now. Guide me and show me the answer to the information I seek."*

Final Declaration

Use at the end of your Sacred Journey and anytime afterwards

Though many fear and come against us from all sides,
Nothing and no one is lost,
All is restored.
Blessed are my ancestors,
Blessed are my kinsmen throughout my family line,
And blessed are my tribesmen.
From generation to generation we reconnect and move as one.
We stretch and move through infinite time and space
We reconnect and work together.
We take heed to learn from past victories and past mistakes
As we reunite, move in unison and work as one,
We are made whole and our strength is restored.
We take charge of our lives and the situations within them
We are truly a blessed and prosperous race.

Diagrams

These are the sketches presented throughout the Sacred Journey Africa text. They are placed here in a larger size which may present a clearer picture than before.

Chapter 11

Prepared bundle cloth

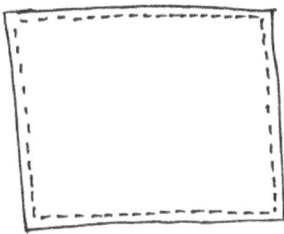

CLOTH SEWN   CLOTH FRINGED

Using cloth to make a bundle for holding items

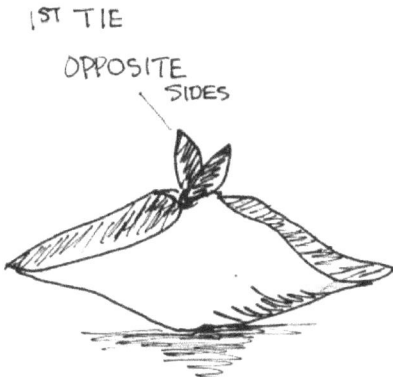

1ST TIE
OPPOSITE
SIDES

2ND TIE
SECOND OPPOSING
SIDES

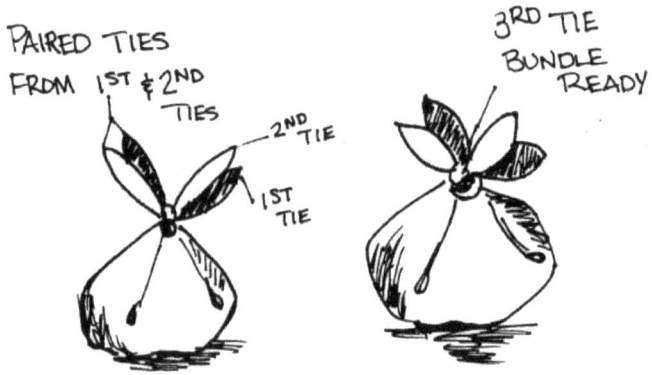

PAIRED TIES FROM 1ST & 2ND TIES
2ND TIE
1ST TIE

3RD TIE BUNDLE READY

Map

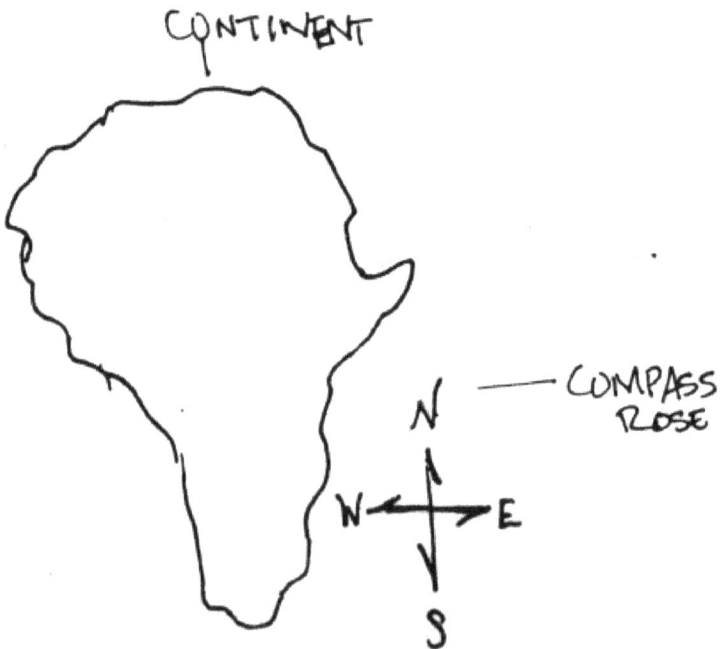

CONTINENT

COMPASS ROSE

N
W E
S

Candles in holders

Candle in alternative holder (foil)

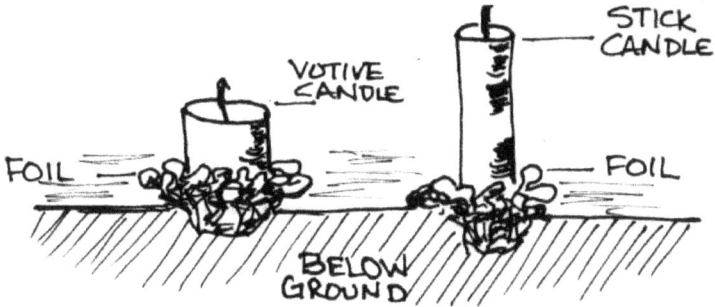

Locator

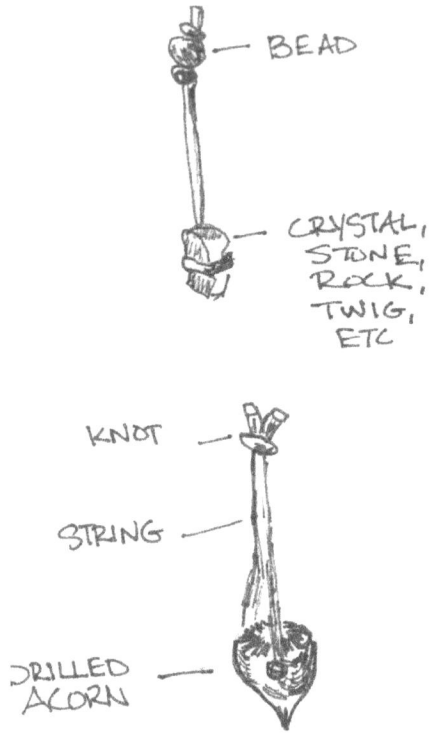

BEAD

CRYSTAL,
STONE,
ROCK,
TWIG,
ETC

KNOT

STRING

DRILLED
ACORN

Chapter 12

Placing name on candle or candle container

Stick, votive, pillar, tea light

ETCHED ON
CONTAINER

ON CANDLE
IN REMOVABLE
CONTAINER

Empowering the candle

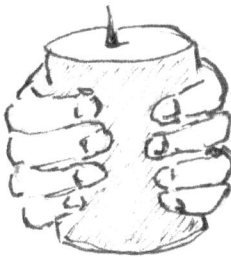

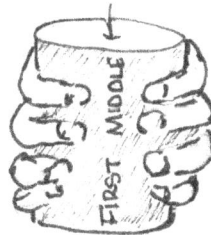

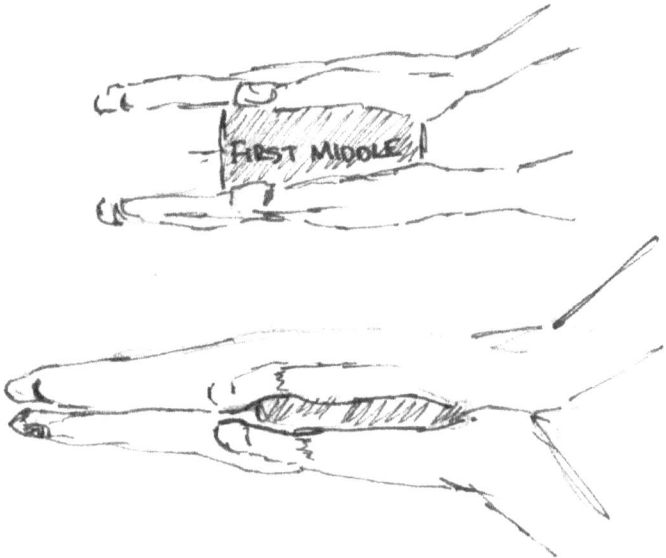

Chapter 14

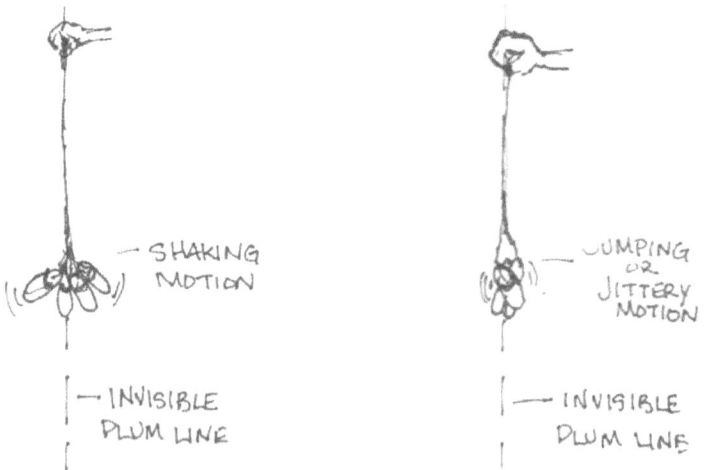

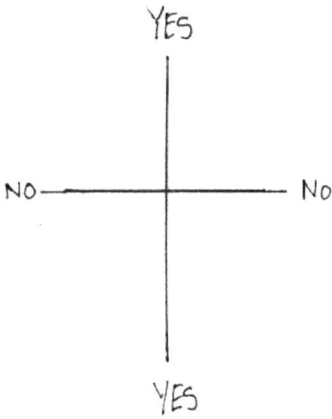

YES

NO — — No

YES

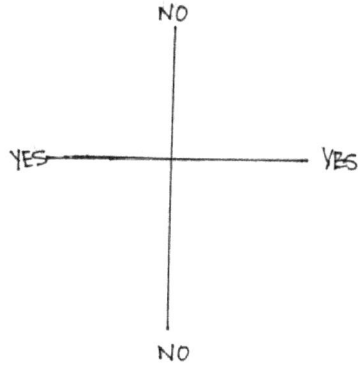

NO

YES — — YES

NO

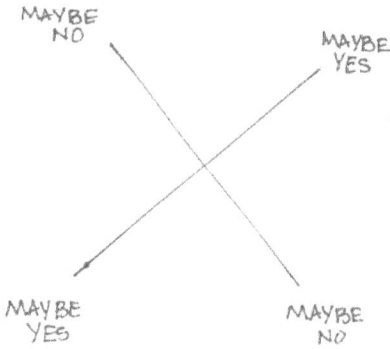

MAYBE
NO

MAYBE
YES

MAYBE
YES

MAYBE
NO

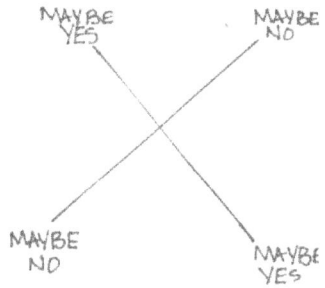

MAYBE
YES

MAYBE
NO

MAYBE
NO

MAYBE
YES

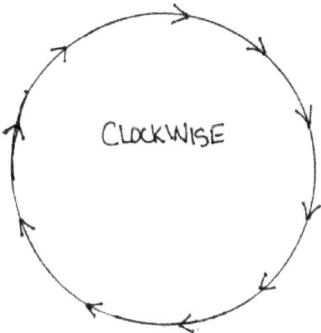

CLOCKWISE

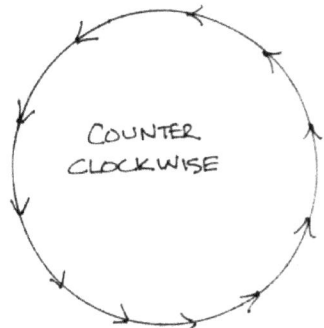

COUNTER
CLOCKWISE

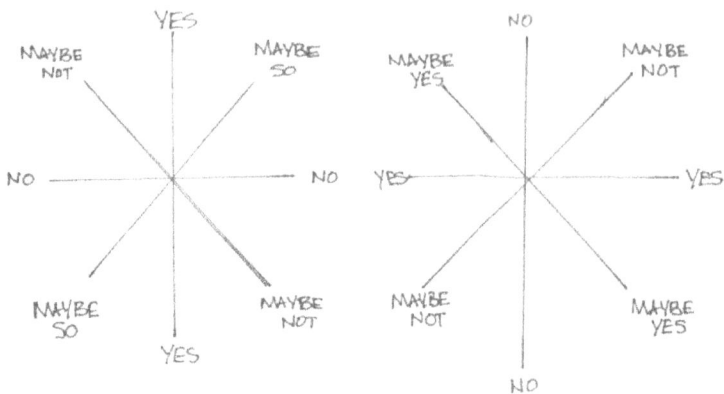

Chapter 16

Measuring the Sacred Space

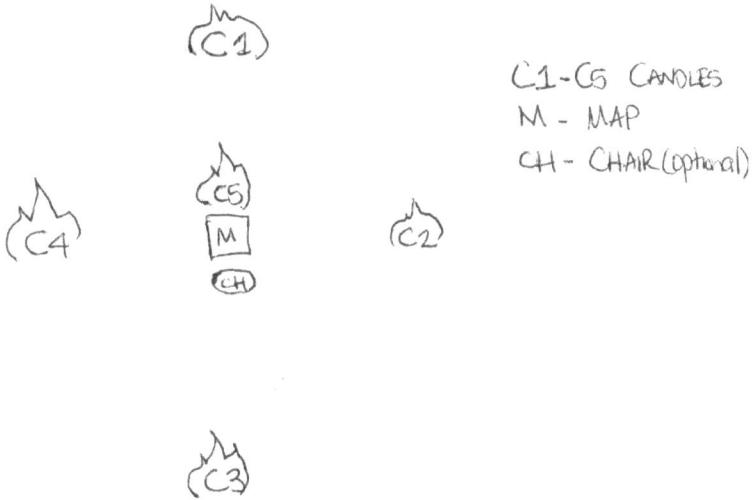

C1-C5 CANDLES
M - MAP
CH - CHAIR (optional)

Sacred space showing chair if needed

Chapter 18

PHASE 1-5

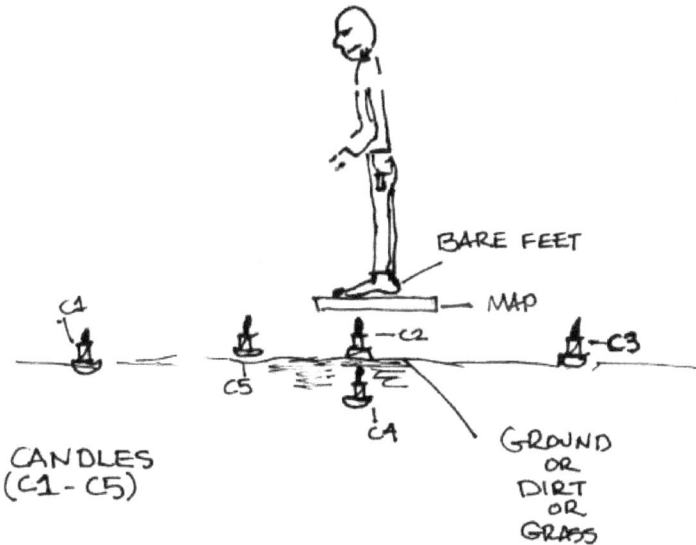

BARE FEET

MAP

C1

C2

C3

C5

C4

CANDLES
(C1- C5)

GROUND
OR
DIRT
OR
GRASS

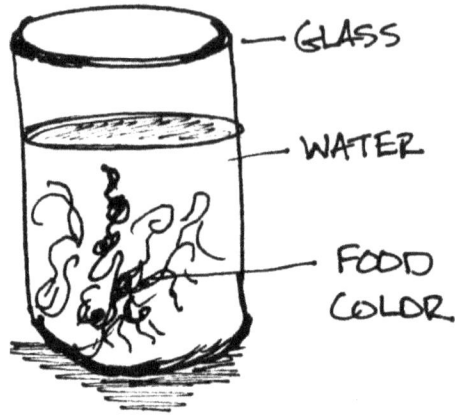

Use glass or bowl

Chapter 19

Alternative Sitting Position

Phase V sitting position

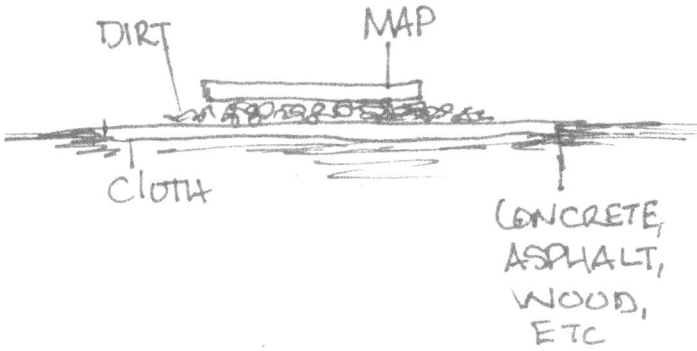

DIRT   MAP

CLOTH

CONCRETE,
ASPHALT,
WOOD,
ETC

When no grass or dirt is present

When partnering with others

Partners facing the same direction

Partners facing different directions

Chapter 21

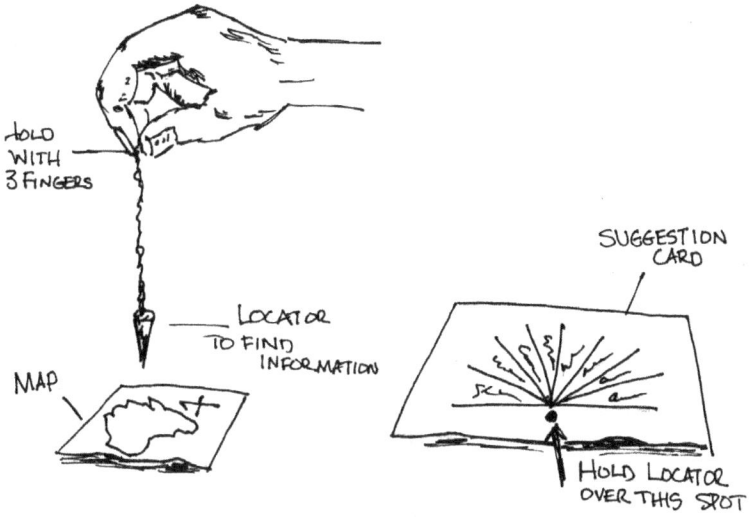

Finding information using Locator

Tugging and pulling of the Pendy

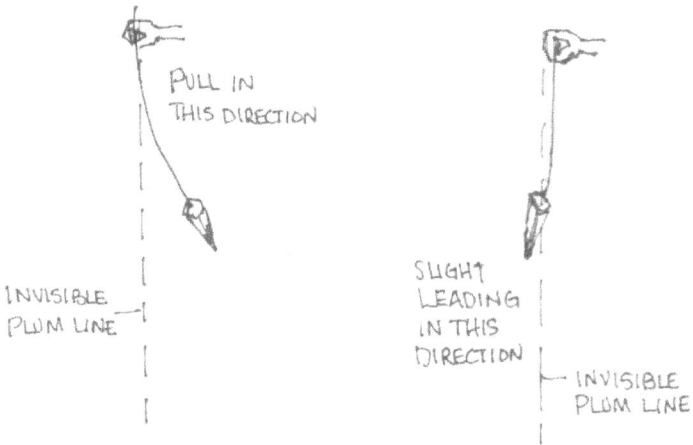

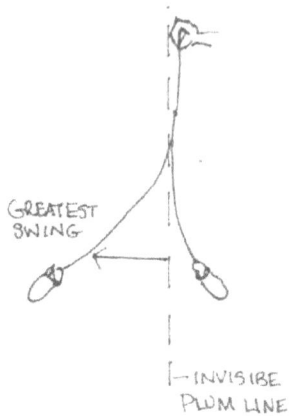

GREATEST
SWING

— INVISIBE
PLUM LINE

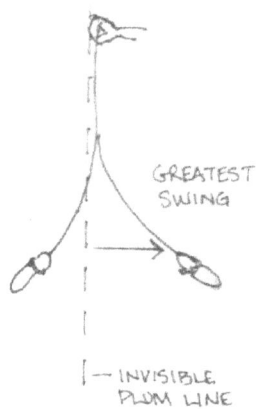

GREATEST
SWING

— INVISIBLE
PLUM LINE

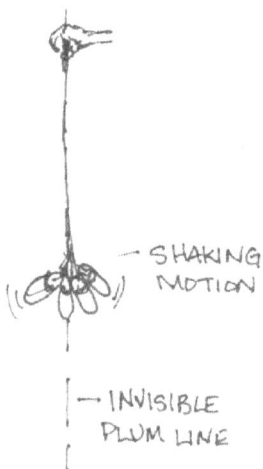

— SHAKING
MOTION

— INVISIBLE
PLUM LINE

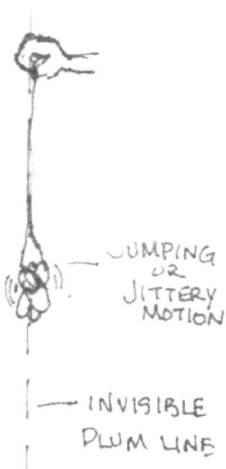

JUMPING
OR
JITTERY
MOTION

— INVISIBLE
PLUM LINE

Glossary

Adverse Energy
Everything is made up of a combination of negative and positive energy. This type of energy can have an overall harmful affect on you or your environment. This is neither good nor bad because everything can be either one according to how it is used. This energy is energy that is not helpful to you. In some cases it will set you back and cause you to just waste time.

Alternative Procedures
These are adaptation to the normal procedures that take into consideration the different living conditions and environments.

Ancestral Family
All of your family members that came before you are your ancestors but within this context we are referring to the members of your family that preceded the Great Rift.

Ancestral Tribe
Your ancestral tribe is a tribe or tribes that your family line descended or came from. The first one you encounter is usually the one at the start of the Great Rift.

Animal Totem(s)
The Universe and other etheric beings use many simple things as a way to communicate with you. Messages are given to you that will help you and guide you along your path. When these come in the form of animals or reptiles they are called Animal Totems. When they appear as sounds, numbers, colors, insect, or aromas they are call Totems.

What makes them Totems is that they are things you would not normally encounter. They seem to just appear then go. If the message is urgent they may jump out at you or reappear until you take notice. You can receive more than one at a time. The time each Totem stays with you varies. There are many books on the subject but as a quick reference take note on the natural habits, behavior, and characteristics of Totem.

Area
There are a total of five of these that together make up one Sacred Journey. You are at liberty to revisit each one to become more comfortable and familiar with them as well as to gain more knowledge about them and yourself. The areas are the Earth, the African Continent, your ancestral tribe, your ancestral family, and Divine Source.

Aromatherapy
Aromatherapy is the practice of using fragrance in the form of oils, plants, flowers, incense, etc as a form of therapy to improve a person's state of health.

Bridge the Gap
Bridging the Gap is the act of connecting like a bridge. This can be people, generations, or time that has been broken, severed, or separated in a manner that does not allow uninterrupted passage, travel, or communication. If a gap in communication, information, or relationships have occurred it causes much to be lost.

Civilized Society
Some people feel a society is civilized according to the dress, activities, progression of technology, and scientific advancements it has made. I would consider it to be one (regardless of its size or location), if it has some type of order, rules set to assist in the well-being of all members. I feel that it can be called civilized if it is an organized functioning society guided by some sense of law and rules that cultivate the well-being, the betterment, and living conditions of those that dwell in it

Cleansing an Item
This is done in order to clear away vibrations that are attached to an item. These could have been attached to an item intentionally or unintentionally by yourself or someone else. They could have also

attached themselves to the object during the manufacturing, processing, or travel.

Cleanse an item with running water (facet, stream, or ocean), placing it in sea salt, prayer, smudging (smoke from sage, lemon, citronella, or other cleansing herb), setting it in sunlight.

Cleansing a Space
The easiest way to cleanse a space or room is to smudge it with smoke from sage lemon, citronella, or other cleansing herb.   If possible you can mop the floor and wipe down the surface areas with lemon, citronella, or ammonia. You can also petition others to do it. Whichever method you choose, open a window or door if possible to allow adverse energies a way out. Direct any adverse energy to leave and return to the Divine to be transformed.

Declarations
A declaration is the process of stating aloud a specific purpose or intention. It is a way of directing oneself in thought and action and getting the Universe to assist you in the stated endeavor. Some people feel more comfortable using a prayer but it is not the same thing. If you ask for help when making a declaration it becomes a prayer or petition (see petitioning).

Dedicating
Declaring aloud, setting an item or space aside for a specific use, and labeling it as such. In doing so you are expressing or announcing it to the Universe and to the universe.

Divine Source
This is God in the purest form. To me God is Divine Infinite, and Source. I often use those terms alone or together. I feel those labels are not restricting and do not in any way place limits on a Being that has no limitations. This Being is in or is part of all things seen or unseen. It is neither male nor female but encompasses both. The beginning DNA of humans is identical until the chromosomes of an embryo make a shift causes the embryo to change. The results then show up as a male or female.

Etheric Beings
This is the same as spiritual beings. It is the spirit, soul, or ghostly nature of a being. Some refer to these beings as God, angels, ascended masters, saints, relatives that have passed on.

Genocidal
This is the systematic erasure of a race of people. A genocidal action is often carried out by means of force, brainwashing, manipulation (gentle or forceful), and through legal as well as illegal means. Gentle manipulation is usually done by enticing or mesmerizing a person so that he or she believes or wants to act in a particular way.

Great Rift
The period of time when many countries captured, enslaved and reprogrammed people from the various tribes that populated the continent of Africa. This is more than what has been called the Contact Zone (meeting & colonization). This is systematic and could be centuries long in time. Countries often sent scouting parties or fleets to the continent to acquire slaves through barter, trade, purchase, or force. They would enslave them through trickery or war. Many times this action would wipeout an entire village or tribe.

Helpers
These are any beings that will come to your aide. These include but or not limited to God, angels, saints, deceased relatives, loved ones, fairies, elves, etc. Helpers can occupy this plane or the etheric plane.

Higher Learning
Higher learning is different from person to person and from country to country. It is the level of education beyond what has been set or determined to be the minimum standard of educational requirements in this country it is levels beyond high school. Our colleges contain several different levels. For some it may mean the level after primary school, high school, technical school, or apprenticeship training.

There are many things in place that will allow a person to attend an institution of higher learning. In most cases people from low-income families are able to receive full funding when seeking a degree. Even if you do not attend a higher learning institute you can still frequent the library or bookstore. There has never been a truer statement made that this: KNOWLEDGE IS POWER.

Holistic Medicine
Holistic medicine is usually a healing art that does not involve processed medicine. It opts to use natural herbs for medicine, natural remedies, energy, acupuncture, meditation etc to bring the body and mind into a balance and whole state of being.

Hominid Like
This is used to describe a being or species that is characteristically human. It said to be those that first took on the look of man but appear bulkier in structural bone mass.

Infinite Being
An Infinite Being is an entity that has no limitations, no beginnings, and no end. It is not bound by any restraints that the mind can place on it.

Kinsmen
These are people that are in your family tree before or after you. They can be any where along the lines of paternal or maternal relatives. You want to first concern yourself with the generation of kinsmen along your maternal line at the time just before the Great Rift began.

Land-locked
This is a physical state of not being located near or having access to a body of water. To many this means a body of water that is tidal and flows. A manmade lake will not suffice.

Locator
A Locator can be any item used to find things or information. It can be handmade using found items, purchased items or a combination of both.

Native

This is a term used to describe a Race of people that has spent their entire known existence in a particular area, state, providence, country, or continent.

Petitioning/Prayer

Petitioning is simply asking others for help. This is done verbally, in writing or a combination of both. For our purposes the others will be etheric beings (see spiritual or Etheric beings), unless you decide you want a sibling to take their Sacred Journey with you. Others ask for help from trees, plants, fairies, elves, etc.

Phase

This is the initial act or part within a session that initializes your connection with a particular area along the Sacred Journey. It involves setting up the space that you will conduct your travel through an area or leg of your Sacred Journey.

Programming Candles

To program a candle means to dedicate it or empower it with an intention for use. This is usually done by making contact with the candle. Contact is made by holding the writing on the candle then holding it while stating the intended use aloud. Any and all thought and intentions should be positive and sincere before, during, and after this action. Oftentimes a purifying bath is done before the programming an object.

Programming Locator

This is a way of developing a simple base for communication between you and the locating object which allows you to exchange information. The traditional answers to questions you pose will be in the form of YES, NO, or MAYBE. You can incorporate MAYBE YES and MAYBE NO as answers if you like.

Purest Information

Pure information is information that is free of fear, added stuff, doctrine, or fillers. It is just the information that is needed and straight from Divine Source. It has not been shaped by biases, beliefs, or religion.

Purifying Bath

A purifying bath is the process of cleansing or preparing oneself. For these purposes you can take a shower or bath. This is done right before you began the programming. During the bath or shower breathe deeply and calmly and tell yourself to release any adverse energy so that you are able to freely move with the Divine. Dry off and proceed with the programming process.

Sacred

This can be any item, action, or thing that is considered special, highly valued, or loved especially if it has a connection with the Divine. Usually links to or enhances your connection to another being, entity, person, time, or God. It is normally set aside from other objects and treated with love and care. Example of this would be an heirloom or religious item.

Sacred Space

A Sacred space has the same inference as Sacred but refers to an area. It is an area or room reserved for special activities. This is usually prayer, intercession, worship, reading of holy writings, or interactions with another person, entity, or God. In cases where a separate area is not available, a temporary area can be created and used. See *Cleansing a Space* for information concerning this.

Selection Card

These are cards that are used in conjunction with a Locator to find information. They can contain information other than YES, NO, and MAYBE. This information allows you to ask questions formulated in a different way. Sometimes it helps you reach an answer quicker. It also allows the Locator to narrow down or point to specific answers.

Session
A session is the time spent exploring an area of Sacred Journey. It can also be seen as the time spent setting up and creating a sacred space and connecting to an area phase).

Spiritual/Spirituality
Spiritual refers to the unseen part of a being. Some believe this to be the spirit, soul, or ghost of a being. These are exchanges through prayer, petitions, speech, actions, or energy that are void of religious antecedents and doctrine. They are usually interactions with the etheric unseen realms between a person and God, past relatives, saints, ascended masters, angels, etc.

Training
Training referred to in this sense was a systematic stripping away of the identity of the people. They were forced to give up everything from their former way of life. This would be the language, clothing, traditions, family connections, and ever their names. This type of training is also known as reprogramming, brainwashing, and colonization.

Tribesmen
These are the people in the tribes that you maternal and paternal kinsmen came from. You want to first concern yourself with the ones that came from the maternal tribe at the time just before the Great Rift began. In some cases the maternal and paternal tribesmen will be the same or from neighboring tribes.

Universal Feminine
This is the creative aspect of God and is found everywhere in the universe. It is the spark that flows to give shape and form to all things. This is neither male nor female in the sexual sense and it is within everything and everyone.

Universe
This refers to God as an Unlimited Infinite Being. This is not the same as universe which is referring to the physical planets, stars, galaxies, etc.

Vibrational Chord

A Vibrational chord is similar to a musical note or chord. When struck it vibrates or resonates over distances in such a way that it can be heard and felt by people or things. It is a frequency at which you can vibrate. Once you are vibrating at it you can connect to the identical chord (in people or things), that resonates through time, space, and dimensions.

Vibrations / Vibrational rate

Everything is made up of molecules and all molecules move at a certain rate of speed. We refer to your overall rate at which you move as your vibrational rate. As you progress through life and interact with the world around you, rate can increase or decrease. It is an invisible gatekeeper that can draw things to you and trigger events.

Bibliography

Africa and the Americas: Culture, Politics, and History, s.v. "African Institution, The," accessed May 01, 2013, https://login .dax.lib.unf.edu/login?qurl=http%3A%2F%2Fwww.cred oreference.com/entry/abcafatrle/African_institution_the

African slave trade [electronic resource]. n.p.: [S.l.] : Magellan Geogra phix, c1997., 1997. UNFeBook Collection, EBSCOhost (accessed April 23, 2013).

Araujo, Ana Lucia. *"Paths of the Atlantic Slave Trade : Interactions, Identities, and Images."* Amherst, N.Y.: Cambria Press, 2011. eBook Collection (EBSCOhost), EBSCOhost (accessed April 23, 2013).

Braiker, Harriet B. 2004. *"Who's Pulling Your Strings? How To Break The Cycle Of Manipulation And Regain Control Of Your Life."* New York: McGraw-Hill. http://search.ebscohost.com/login .aspx?direct=true&scope=site&db=nlebk&db=nlabk&AN= 99803.United States, and Edward Hunter. *Communist psychologi cal warfare (brainwashing)*. Washington: U.S. Government Print ing Office. 1958.

Britain and the Americas: Culture, Politics, and History, s.v. "Slave Trade, Atlantic," accessed May 01, 2013, https://login.dax.lib.unf .edu/login?qurl=http%3A%2F%2Fwww.credoreference.com /entry/abcbramrle/slave_trade_atlantic

Carruthers, Susan L. *"Cold War Captives: Imprisonment, Escape, And Brainwashing."* Berkeley: University of California Press. 2009.

Encyclopedia of African History, s.v. "Egypt, Ancient: Hieroglyphics and Origins of Alphabet," accessed May 01, 2013, https://login .dax.lib.unf.edu/login?qurl=http%3A%2F%2Fwww.credore ference.com/entry/routafricanhistory/egypt_ancient_hierogl yphics_and_origins_of_alphabet

Encyclopedia of Archaeology: History and Discoveries, s.v. "Africa, South, Prehistory," accessed May 01, 2013, https://login.dax.lib.unf .edu/login?qurl=http%3A%2F%2Fwww.credoreference.com /entry/abcarch/africa_south_prehistory

Encyclopedia of Archaeology, s.v. "Europe, Eastern, Peopling Of,"
        accessed May 01, 2013, https://login.dax.lib.unf.edu/login?
        qurl=http%3A%2F%2Fwww.credoreference.com/entry/
        estarch/europe_eastern_peopling_of
Encyclopedia of Emancipation and Abolition in the Transatlantic World, s.v.
        "Federal Writers' Project, Slave Narrative Collection,"
         Accessed May 01, 2013,https://login.dax.lib.unf.edu/
        login?qurl=http%3A%2F%2Fwww.credoreference.com/entr
        y/sharpeeman/federal_writers_project_slave_narrative_colle
        ction
Encyclopedia of the Antebellum South, s.v. "Punishment of Slaves,"
        accessed May 01, 2013,https://login.dax.lib.unf.edu/
        login?qurl=http%3A%2F%2Fwww.credoreference.com/entr
        y/abcas/punishment_of_slaves
Encyclopedia of the United States in the Nineteenth Century, s.v. "Slavery,"
        accessed May 01, 2013, ttps://login.dax.lib.unf.edu/login?qur
        l=http%3A%2F%2Fwww.credoreference.com/entry/galeus/
        slavery
Encyclopedia of World Trade From Ancient Times to the Present, s.v.
        "Cuneiform," accessed May 01, 2013, ttps://login.dax.lib.unf
        .edu/login?qurl=http%3A%2F%2Fwww.credoreference.com
        /entry/sharpewt/cuneiform
Enroth, Ronald M. *"Youth, Brainwashing, And The Extremist Cults."*
        Grand Rapids: Zondervan Pub. House. 1977.
Forward, Susan, and Donna Frazier. *"Emotional Blackmail: When The
        People In Your Life Use Fear, Obligation, And Guilt To Manipulate
        You."* New York, NY: HarperCollins Publishers. 1997.
Goff, Kenneth. *"Brain-washing: a Synthesis of the Russian Textbook On
        Psychopolitics."* [s.l.: s.n., 1960.
Human Evolution: A Guide to the Debates, s.v. "Africa," accessed May
        01, 2013, https://login.dax.lib.unf.edu/login?qurl=http
        %3A%2F%2Fwww.credoreference.com/entry/abcregale/
        africa
Washburn, Sherwood., Elwyn Simons, John Napier."et.al". *Scientific
        American: Human Ancestors.* San Francisco, C.A.: W. H.
        Freeman and Company. 1979.

Jayasuriya, Shihan de S. *The African Diaspora in Asian Trade Routes and Cultural Memories.* Lewiston, N.Y.: Edwin Mellen Press, 2010. eBook Collection (EBSCOhost), BSCOhost (accessed April 23, 2013).

Jews and the Civil War: A Reader, s.v. "Jews and Negro Slavery in the Old South, 1789-1865," accessed May 01, 2013, https://login.dax.lib.unf.edu/login?qurl=http%3A%2F%2Fwww.credoreference.com/entry/nyupjcwar/jews_and_negro_slavery_in_the_old_south_1789-1865

Meerloo, Joost Abraham Maurits. *"The rape of the mind; the psychology of thought control, menticide, and brainwashing."* New York: Grosset & Dunlap. 1961.

Nigeria's Diverse Peoples: A Reference Sourcebook, s.v. "European Contact and the Atlantic Slave Trade," accessed May)1, 2013, ttps://login.dax.lib.unf.edu/login?qurl=http%3A%2F%2Fwww.credoreference.com/entry/abcnigeria/european_contact_and_the_atlantic_slave_trade

Philip's Encyclopedia 2008, s.v. "hieroglyphics," accessed May 01, 2013, https://login.dax.lib.unf.edu/login?qurl=http%3A%2F%2Fwww.credoreference.com/entry/philipency/hieroglyphics

Slavery in the United States: A Social, Political, and Historical Encyclopedia, s.v. "Domestic Slave Trade," accessed May 01, 2013, https://login.dax.lib.unf.edu/login?qurl=http%3A%2F%2Fwww.credoreference.com/entry/abcslavery/domestic_slave_trade

The Crystal Reference Encyclopedia, s.v. "slave trade," accessed May 01, 2013, https://login.dax.lib.unf.edu/login?qurl=http%3A%2F%2Fwww.credoreference.com/entry/cre/slave_trade

The Hutchinson Unabridged Encyclopedia with Atlas and Weather Guide, s.v. "Human Species, Origins of," accessed May 01, 2013, https://login.dax.lib.unf.edu/login?qurl=http%3A%2F%2Fwww.credoreference.com/entry/heliconhe/human_species_origins_of

The Macmillan Encyclopedia, s.v. "Cuneiform," accessed May 01, 2013, https://login.dax.lib.unf.edu/login?qurl=http%3A%2F%2Fwww.credoreference.com/entry/move/cuneiform

The World of Child Labor: An Historical and Regional Survey, s.v. "Section 2 South America," accessed May 01, 2013, https://login.dax .lib.unf.edu/login?qurl=http%3A%2F%2Fwww.credo reference.com/entry/sharpecl/section_2_south_america

Tibbles, Anthony. "Facing Slavery's Past: The Bicentenary of the Abolition of the British Slave Trade." *Slavery & Abolition* 29, no. 2 (June 2008): 293-303. Academic Search Complete, EBSCOhost (accessed April 23, 2013).

Sacred Journey Africa Workbook

This is a companion workbook for Sacred Journey Africa. It alleviates the need to use a journal. This companion workbook has plenty of room for you to jot down notes, sketches, and important information that you receive while on your Sacred Journey.

The workbook has area prompts to help you maneuver with ease through each area of your Sacred Journey. You can learn how to work more effectively with a Locator and make detailed selection cards. You can use this fabulous workbook to plot migration and trade routes and other interactions with neighboring tribes. You are able to write down and keep track of everything in one place.

The information you gleam while on your Sacred Journey is too valuable to forget or lose. You can use the Sacred Journey Africa Workbook to help you create something you can treasure and pass on to others in your family.

Projected publication date: Summer 2014
Size: 8x10
Pages: 100+
ISBN: 0-9764387-7-1
ISBN13:   978-0-9764387-7-9

Sacred Journey Africa-Reclaiming Your Ancestral Heritage

Sacred Journey Africa-Reclaiming Your Ancestral Heritage

Sacred Journey Africa-Reclaiming Your Ancestral Heritage

Sacred Journey Africa-Reclaiming Your Ancestral Heritage

www.ingramcontent.com/pod-product-compliance
Lightning Source LLC
Chambersburg PA
CBHW071222290326
41931CB00037B/1854